A WINTER IN INDIA

A WINTER IN INDIA

THE RT. HON. W. E. BAXTER, M. P.

GYAN

Published by

Gyan Publishing House
5, Ansari Road
Daryaganj, New Delhi-110002
Phone: 011-47034999, 9811692060
E-mail: books@gyanbooks.com

Distribution Network
gyanbooks.com
India, USA, Canada, UK, Australia, France

ISBN: 978-81-212-8376-2 (PB)
First Published, 1882

2nd Impression 2023

Printed at: Gyan Press, Delhi.

A WINTER IN INDIA
Author: W. E. BAXTER

A WINTER IN INDIA.

KINCHINJUNGA RANGE, FROM TIGER HILL, ABOVE DARJEELING.

A

WINTER IN INDIA.

BY

THE RT. HON. W. E. BAXTER, M.P.

With Map and Illustrations.

CASSELL, PETTER, GALPIN & CO.:
LONDON, PARIS & NEW YORK.

1882.

To my Wife: MY COURAGEOUS COMPANION DURING MANY JOURNEYS IN EUROPE, ASIA, AFRICA, AND AMERICA: THESE LEAVES FROM MY INDIAN JOURNAL

ARE AFFECTIONATELY DEDICATED.

CONTENTS.

LIST OF ILLUSTRATIONS.

From Sketches by ROSA ELIZABETH BAXTER.

A WINTER IN INDIA.

CHAPTER I.

THE VOYAGE OUT.

AGAIN we are on the move, and this time for a more extended tour even than that which we so much enjoyed through Egypt and Syria.

We have taken eight first-class and two second-class return tickets in the P. and O. steamers to India.

On the 2nd November, 1881, our old friend the *Wave* took us across the Channel; the Belgians politely passed our baggage at the frontiers without examination; and we remained all night at the Grand Hotel, in Brussels, situated between the two railway stations, thus avoiding the usual climb to the top of the hill.

Next day we went on to Coblentz, passing by in the morning hundreds of fields, from which the peasants were busy removing beet-root to the sugar factories. At Herbesthal the German custom-house officers, "dressed in a little brief authority," made themselves so unpleasant in rummaging our valises that I considered it my duty to write in the evening to the proper quarter complaining of their conduct. At Cologne we had an hour to look at the cathedral, the towers of which are now completed. The Hôtel Belle Vue, at Coblentz, commands a fine view of Ehrenbreitstein and the drawbridge across the Rhine, the latter crowded with passengers and vehicles, and opened every few minutes to allow steamers and barges to pass. We spent the next night at the clean, bustling, thriving, and picturesque town of Wurtzburg, having crossed the "blue Franconian mountains," and on the following day passed over an uninteresting plain to Munich, remaining all Sunday in the Hôtel of the Four Seasons.

On Monday morning we were provided with a handsome saloon carriage, in which we travelled all the way to Venice. In some parts of the

Bavarian plain the peasants were making hay, which I certainly had not seen before in November. The weather hitherto had been very cold, but fortunately we had a lovely day to cross the Brenner Pass, and I never saw the glorious scenery of the Tyrol, the noble entrance to the Inn valley, its startling peaks, gorges, and precipices, to such advantage. Then there was a bright moon to lighten the valley of the Adige, and enable us to walk as if by day to the Grand Hotel at Trent, where we spent the night.

On the following day we had four hours at Verona, to get luncheon and see the place, and it was very late before we reached the City of the Waters, as a locomotive had broken down at Peschiera, detaining the train from Milan. How bright and beautiful is Venice, and what a contrast between its stirring appearance now and the dead city under Austrian domination which I knew in 1844!

At 10 a.m. on 11th November we went on board the P. and O. steamer *Mongolia*, Captain Thompson, 2,833 tons, lying in the Guidecca; and the first person that addressed me on the deck was Sir A. H. Layard, who has a house in Venice, and who was seeing off another old friend of mine, Sir W. Gregory, formerly Member for Galway, and more recently Governor of Ceylon. We had likewise on board Mr. Rowsell, once head of the Contract Department at the Admiralty, and now one of the Commissioners of the State Lands in Egypt, with his family; and I soon found out among the passengers several gentlemen connected with Eastern commerce whose reputation and firms I knew. The *Mongolia* was very high in the water, and as we "slowed" down the Lido passage into the Adriatic, I thought I had never seen anything so beautiful of their kind as the varied views of Venice from the sea. By nightfall we were off Ancona, burning blue lights on the port bow; and so calm was the sometimes stormy gulf that by 1 a.m. on Sunday we were standing in and out at Brindisi, waiting for the pilot, who was in bed. The ship is manned chiefly by natives of the East, who go under the general designation of Lascars, most of whom come from the islands and headlands to the north of

Bombay, and we have a considerable number of passengers on board for Australia. The Rev. Mr. Mitchell, of Sydney, conducted divine service in the saloon after we had finished the dirty operation of coaling. I never saw a more squalid, filthy, rickety-looking place than the ancient Brundusium ; but it has a good harbour, and probably at some future time it will be more inviting to the traveller.

At 2 o'clock on Monday morning the train came in, wearied railway passengers rushed into the cabins, and very soon heavy rolling warned me that we were once more on the Adriatic. When I went on deck in the morning, Otranto, on the Italian coast, was in full view, and opposite, crowned with snow, appeared the lofty mountains of Albania. Passing Cape Matapan, distinctly visible though thirty miles off, we had run 289 miles at noon, and until we got under the lee of Crete the good ship plunged so much that many of the passengers were sick for four or five hours.

Wednesday was a lovely day, and when I reached the deck at sunrise on Thursday, in the lurid light on the eastern horizon there could be plainly seen a dim object familiar to me—the Pharos of Alexandria. The usual din and scramble took place when the steamer stopped in the inner harbour; but we did not require to land in boats, as the P. and O. Company have now got a wharf, and the railway carriages come down to the steamer's side. For an additional payment of £1 each, we shared with others a large saloon carriage, and regretfully saying good-bye to the *Mongolia*, were soon passing between Lake Mareotis and the Mahmudieh Canal, among fields of cotton, maize, rice, and reeds; camels, buffaloes, and naked Arabs reminding us of former times.

This is Thursday, 17th November, 1881, and on the same day of the week and month in 1869 was opened the Suez Canal—a monument of French enterprise and sagacity which England's short-sighted statesmen had so long and so foolishly opposed.

The rascals charged us four shillings each for a very so-so lunch at Kafr Zayad, and we were not sorry when the hot and dusty journey terminated at Suez at 9 p.m., and we were ushered into the saloon of the steamship *Surat*, Captain Breeze, 3,142 tons, where all that the P. and O. Company could provide for weary and hungry passengers was a supper of very bad and tough cold meat.

The luncheons of that generous corporation are cold; and although the order, and especially the cleanliness, on board are all that can be desired, a company that charge so high and enjoy so large a subsidy from Government should supply better fare and provide faster steamers. There is nothing to prevent the service between London and Bombay being shortened by at least three days.

The *Surat*, although she performed admirably while we were on board, has been rather an unfortunate ship, and has met with a good many mishaps. In 1875 we saw her disabled and being towed in the Suez Canal, and this voyage her engines stopped five times in the Bay of Biscay, so alarming the passengers that they applied to the captain of the port and Lord Napier of Magdala at Gibraltar for an independent examination of the machinery, greatly to the indignation of the chief engineer and of the captain. We consequently found by no means a happy family on board, and we heard much of their experiences and grievances during the passage.

Next day we were going thirteen knots with a fresh northerly breeze between the magnificent serrated peaks which hide Sinai from view, and the almost equally striking mountains on the African coast. We met six steamers going up to Suez. The ship is full, there being 130 first-class passengers, whose easy-chairs cover the quarter-deck.

Passing Shadwan Island, where the P. and O. steamship *Carnatic* was lost, we leave the Gulf of Suez, and, seeing the entrance to the Gulf of Akaba on the left, pass into the Red Sea, or, as it should be called, the Sea of Sea-weed, the Hebrew word for the two being the same. A wreck standing well out of the water reminds us of the dangers of its navigation. The mountains on both sides are much grander than I imagined, and, as we proceed, those on the

African shore present a most remarkable appearance, as if cut into gigantic steps. We have volunteer music on deck every evening at 8.30 —piano-playing, songs and glees.

Saturday, 19th, was quite calm. We are out of sight of land, but pass the solitary light on the shoal where H.M.S. *Dædalus* was lost. I am surprised at the number of people on board going, like ourselves, merely to travel in India, and not on official duty or commercial business. The thermometer has stood steadily at 80°. Now the temperature rises. At 8 o'clock on Sunday morning it was 86° in the shade on the companion, and few people had been able to sleep from the heat. At 10.30 a.m. all hands were mustered in their Sunday dress on the quarter-deck, and at 10.45 a young chaplain going out to Delhi conducted divine service.

The colour of the Red Sea is a lapis-lazuli blue. Our run was 294 miles, and at 3 p.m. the thermometer in the shade registered 95°, and very little walking was done on deck. Small sails were put out from each cabin window, to make a draught, and the punkahs in the saloon were kept hard at work. Not a rock, or a steamer, or a light-house was to be seen.

On Monday the *Surat* had a very unusual experience: namely, a strong head-wind, a tempestuous sea, and 96° of heat in the shade. Most people were motionless, and looked very miserable. The ports had all to be closed, and ladies slept on the saloon table and all about the place. We were shipping such heavy seas that the captain had to slacken speed during the night. In the evening we passed the Island of Jebeltur, and here the navigation is not a little ticklish.

There are two other Members of Parliament on board, going to see India—my friend Mr. Hamilton, of South Lanarkshire, and Mr. Johnson, who represents Exeter. We have a considerable number of British officers returning from furlough, men of large experience and cultivation; and I am happy to find that most of them are by no means Jingoes, and that some who approved of the Afghan expedition are now convinced that it was a terrible mistake. A friend tells me that he went home recently with twenty-eight officers of the Cabul force, twenty-five of whom informed him that they approved of the evacuation of Candahar.

We are now in full sight of the Arabian coast, with Mocha in the distance, a strong wind dead ahead. The Straits of Babel Mandeb, or "The Gate of Tears"—so called from the number of wrecks that have taken place on that desolate shore—are 14 miles wide, and the Island of Perim, on which flies the British flag, lying right in the channel commands the entrance to the Red Sea. It is only two miles distant from a very striking promontory on the Arabian coast, and we ran through that narrow passage, meeting the steamship *City of Agra* under full sail going north, and two other steamers also taking advantage of the wind just outside on the Indian Ocean.

By 11 p.m. we were at anchor in the wonderful harbour of Aden, but the noise made by coaling, and by the naked Soumali boys diving for coins, prevented much sleep. When I came on deck I found it crowded with natives selling ostrich feathers, baskets, and other articles. We were anchored between a French man of war, and the P. and O. steamer *Assam*, from Bombay. The Italian gunboat *Chioggia* passed up harbour under our stern, and by-and-bye the great P. and O. steamer *Nepaul* arrived from Calcutta.

Aden surprised me; it is as fine as Gibraltar, and has a splendid anchorage. The wild barren rocks and peaks dotted over with white houses present a singular appearance, and it is a much more imposing place than I had imagined. We lay there till nearly 10 o'clock on Wednesday morning, and might have gone ashore, but a placard announcing that the ship was to sail at 5 a.m. prevented us. The cantonments, which are five miles from the harbour, can be seen very distinctly from the sea after leaving.

Lofty mountains in Arabia were visible all Wednesday afternoon and Thursday morning. I learned to-day that in the Red Sea on Sunday the thermometer in the stoke-hole was 154°. We have several excellent artists on board, and people who fall asleep in ungraceful attitudes, especially when they are not prepossessing, find themselves immortalised in sketch-books.

On Monday night the quarter-deck was decorated with flags, and we had a ball, which was kept up for several hours. At 2.30 a.m. on Tuesday I happened to look out of my port-hole, and there, in all its glory, just above the horizon, was the Southern Cross: and certainly my feeling on seeing it for the first time was by no means one of disappointment.

Between 6 and 7 o'clock I went to the bow, and saw the land—peaks in the Ghauts on each side of Bombay. The colour of the water is changed to a light dirty brown; a row of fishing-boats stationed right in the way of the navigation—why, I don't know, nor it appears does anyone else—are on the starboard; and right ahead, one by one begin to appear the spires and factory chimneys of the city.

CHAPTER II.

BOMBAY—THE RAJPOOTANA RAILWAY.

BEFORE nine we had taken the pilot on board, and then the *Surat* wound her way up one of the finest harbours in the world, the capaciousness and grand scenery of which took me quite by surprise; and as soon as she dropped anchor a steam-launch came alongside with a letter from the Viceroy in camp, welcoming me in the kindest and most cordial terms to the shores of India; and another from the Governor of Bombay, to take our party ashore if we desired it. We landed, however, in boats provided by business correspondents. The noise, scramble, and heat were what the Americans would call "a caution."

Stepping ashore at the celebrated quay called Apollo Bunder, the evening resort of the beauty and fashion of Bombay, we drove at once to the Cumballa family hotel on Cumballa Hill, a quiet villa which has the advantage of a northern

VIEW FROM CUMBALLA HILL BOMBAY.

aspect and breeze. This Orient is quite different from that which I had seen before; nearly all the trees are new to me, and excepting the poinsettias and bougainvilleas, I do not recognise the flowers. The houses are bungalows, and the manners and customs of the strangely-attired, or rather non-attired, natives strongly impress on us that our time is six hours earlier than that of Greenwich.

I was not prepared for the magnificence of the view of the city and its surroundings from Malabar Hill—the sea of palms, the noble public buildings, the bays and creeks, the peaked and dome-shaped Ghauts; it has a resemblance to the Bay of Naples, but there is more variety, and the mountains are further off. At night there were marriage festivities in the neighbourhood, music and fireworks, preventing some of the party sleeping until the small hours.

On the top of Malabar Hill, and within sight of our windows, are the Towers of Silence: a walled cemetery where dead Parsees are devoured by vultures; and you see those hideous creatures gorged and sleepy on every tree.

We had a most delightful excursion in the afternoon in a steam-launch, one hour from the harbour to the celebrated caves of Elephanta; and the beauty of the sunset on the bay, peaks and islands, port and shipping, can never be forgotten. Then in the evening some of us were entertained to dinner in the Yacht Club. It is a fine airy erection on the Apollo Bunder, now called the Wellington pier, so well ventilated that punkahs are not required; and everything was served just as it would be in the "Carlton" or "Reform."

The stranger is struck with the great number of policemen stationed along all the streets and roads, who touch their hats to every sahib who passes; and the crowds of servants in every house and counting-house, moving noiselessly about like shadows, impress a European.

It is a very pretty drive to the Government House at the furthest point of Malabar Hill, past innumerable bungalows of merchants and officials—Scotch names greatly predominating—the strange trees and flowers reminding one forcibly how far he is from home.

We dined in one of these sumptuous villas, and the *appétit* was the fitful glare from Hindoo bodies being cremated on the other side of the bay. Notwithstanding the howling of the jackals, we had music and song before returning home in the moonlight.

I experienced considerable difficulty next day in arranging both about travelling servants and money; and it is no joke walking along the streets of the Fort under a burning sun, even although your head is protected by a pith helmet; but then we are rewarded by the glorious view of mountains, bay, and shipping from the restaurant on the quay: I never saw anything of the kind more lovely.

The municipality of Bombay is partly elective and partly nominative; the majority are natives, and they manage economically and well. I observed how carefully kept, repaired, and watered are all the thoroughfares.

It is impossible to convey in a few sentences of description anything like a vivid idea of this strange Bombay. The mixture of splendid public buildings and hovels, sumptuous bungalows cheek-by-jowl with wigwams, carriages and ox-carts, men with bare feet sitting in broughams attended by liveried servants, shops full of nearly naked people, women flitting about in garments of dazzling brightness, with jewels in their noses, bracelets on their ankles, and rings on their toes; tramways, cotton bales, bheesties pressing water out of their pigskins to lay the dust; people of every nation, kindred, and tongue. More than 700,000 souls crowded in narrow lanes form a *tout ensemble* which to be realised must be seen.

The traveller in India has to provide himself with quilts and pillows, for use both in the railway carriages and in the däk bungalows or houses provided for the accommodation of travellers. With this addition to our baggage we mingled with a motley crew in Grant Road Station, waiting for the mail train which had started from the harbour half an hour before, on Saturday evening, December 3rd, at 5.30.

It soon became dark, but in the bright moonlight we could see pretty well around. The line crosses from the Island of Bombay to the mainland by a very long viaduct, and there are a great many other bridges over various arms of the sea. Before turning in for the night, we came in view of a fine range of peaked mountains; and were soon reminded, in our endeavours to draw our quilts more closely around us, that it is now no longer excessively hot, but on the contrary rather cold.

The first thing I saw when day dawned was a troop of huge monkeys making faces at the train, running up trees, and turning somersaults for our edification.

At Ahmedabad we had a good breakfast, and changed into the carriages of the narrow-gauge Rajpootana State Railway. This interposition of a line of different width between the other great railroads in India appears to me to be a blunder, and one which must eventually be remedied, no matter what may be the cost.

During the forenoon we passed through fields of maize, rice, cotton, and castor-oil, separated by cactus hedges, and saw many large herds of cattle and buffaloes. The peasants were very busy ploughing and irrigating; most of them were nearly or quite naked, and inhabited miserable-looking huts. There were raised look-out posts, sometimes on a framework, sometimes on a tree, here and there, with watchers to prevent the deer, boars, monkeys, and other wild animals damaging the crops. The station houses and the dwellings of the better class have all white domes like mosques.

During this day and the following morning I saw more wild creatures, four-footed and winged, than I ever saw during the same period in all my life—deer and monkeys of various sizes and kinds, cockatoos innumerable, blue jays, flamingoes, storks of the most graceful appearance, partridges, jungle-fowl, doves, and water-birds in endless variety—nowhere in India is there finer shooting than in Rajpootana, as well in the jungles as in the desert, of both of which we had samples during our journey. Towards evening we passed between two very striking ranges, that of Mount Aboo on the left being 5,000 feet high; and we had a glorious sunset illuminating their jagged peaks.

Did not we bless the promoters of the narrow-gauge line during the hours of darkness? A night on the Rajpootana State Railway! What a reminiscence! To roughly-made carriages was added a bad locomotive-driver, and the jerking, pitching, and rolling overtask my feeble powers of description. The water-cistern in our saloon carriage was broken, my clothes were hurled on the sloppy floor, holding on for dear life was impossible, because there was nothing to hold by. I got up to put the quilt over me, and was banged head foremost against my *vis-à-vis*. Natives yelled at our ears the names of every station, and it was not till day dawned beyond Ajmere that we got a little broken rest. This was our first experience of luxurious railway travelling in India; many times I tried, Christian-like, to laugh, but it seemed much more natural and easy to do the other thing.

At Phalera junction in the early morning I got out for a cup of tea, and was amazed to be addressed on the platform by Mr. Primrose, private secretary to the Viceroy, formerly my private secretary at the Treasury, who had joined the train during the night. Truly thankful we were after forty-two hours' shaking on that dreadful line to take refuge in the dâk bungalow at Jeypoor. Colonel Bannerman, the Political Resident at the Maharajah's capital, had arranged it for our reception, and sent carriages to meet us at the station.

It is a square bungalow in the centre of a compound. There are reed huts for the servants on one side, and on the other tents, in case of an overflow of guests, reminding us of our life in Palestine.

Attended by a gorgeous man in red, we called on the Resident in his beautiful villa in the neighbourhood, and then drove through the extraordinary town of Jeypoor—a mixture of Orientalism and European innovation hard to describe. There are broad streets; houses, higher than usual, all painted pink; a vast palace, half a mile long and eight stories high; a well laid-out and beautifully-kept public garden, in which the dons of the city were taking their evening ride; runners to warn the crowds in the streets of the approach of the sahibs;

STREET IN JEYPOOR.

monkeys scrambling over the house-tops; bheesties making the water squirt in every direction —altogether it was like a scene in the Arabian Nights.

We had a quiet dinner in the bungalow; there was an eclipse of the moon in that glorious star-lit sky, and we said good-night amidst a howling of the jackals far more deafening than any we had experienced in Egypt.

The stranger is struck at this time of year by the withered and burnt-up appearance of the whole country. Vast tracts on the plains are covered with the graceful pampas-grass, which is collected for purposes of thatching.

A large party had assembled at the Residency to dinner, consisting chiefly of officers from Bombay, who had come up to enjoy the sport of pig-sticking; and we had much conversation on many interesting points connected with Indian affairs.

The air next morning was quite frosty, and I felt even an ulster insufficient to keep out the cold, as we set off in carriages at a hand-gallop to visit Amber, the old capital of the state: a most extraordinary place, situated in a hollow, the lofty hills surrounding it being fortified somewhat in the fashion of Verona. After a drive of four miles, we found elephants waiting us, and had our first experience of riding in a howdah. I thought the motion more unpleasant, but not so difficult for a tyro, than that of being on the back of a camel.

From various points on the roof of the Maharajah's palace we obtained very remarkable and extensive views of the surrounding country.

The Rajpoots of old were freebooters and thieves, like the Scottish chiefs, and their towns had to be built for purposes of defence.

During our absence one of our servants saw the execution of a dacoit, who was brought out of the town in an ox-cart, and strung up close to the gate of the bungalow. The carriages and elephants have all been placed at our disposal by the Maharajah.

Several successive rulers of Jeypoor have been enlightened, reforming men. The beautiful Mayo hospital, the water-supply to the town, and the irrigation works in the vicinity are some of the monuments of good government in this little state. There are about 100,000 inhabitants in the capital, which is commanded by the Tiger Fort, on the top of a lofty hill.

While I was sitting in the verandah of the bungalow, in the afternoon, I was surprised and pleased to receive a visit from the Rev. John Traill, a Brechin man, who has been nine years connected with the United Presbyterian Mission in Rajpootana, and who, I afterwards learnt, is not only respected by the whole European community, but is such a favourite among the natives that all classes delight to receive and listen to him.

Shortly after 8 o'clock on Thursday morning we were off again on the State railway; and although the travelling was certainly much smoother than between Ahmedabad and Ajmere, it was by no means what it ought to be, and I cannot find anyone hereabouts who has now a good word to say for the metre gauge. It is what the Americans call an air line, or nearly straight, as far as Bandikui, passing partly over great grassy wastes, inhabited by deer and parroquets and peacocks, and partly through fields of grain and cotton, the former of which the peasants were busy irrigating from numerous wells.

The only town of any importance on this route is Alwur, with 50,000 inhabitants, the capital of another Rajpoot state.

CHAPTER III.

DELHI AND LAHORE.

AND now I write in Delhi, the ancient capital of the Great Mogul, historically celebrated in many ways, and the scene of events in the Mutiny of 1857 which shook the British dominion in Hindostan to its very base, and horrified and excited the whole civilised world. Sixty-six officers and 1,100 men fell in that terrible final assault, which once more vindicated our supremacy over a population of 300 millions, and enables Queen Victoria now to grant patents of accession to no fewer than 153 native princes.

We have plucked a leaf from that banyan-tree inside the fort where twenty-seven Europeans were massacred in cold blood; and we have wondered and admired in the lovely private audience-hall—a garden of roses on one hand, and on the other the river Jumna, with the great railway-bridge. It is a pavilion of white marble, which once contained the famous Peacock Throne, where the puppet emperor resided during the siege, and where the Prince of Wales received in durbar the magnates of India. The ladies' apartments are now the officers' mess-room, and the audience-chamber of Shah Jehan has been converted into the canteen of the British force!

Since the Mutiny, all the buildings near the fort—which itself is one-and-a-quarter miles in circumference—have been demolished, and the space has been laid out in walks and trees. We entered it by the Lahore Gate, where there is a row of native shops, for the benefit of the soldiers—"Ram Sing, tailor," &c.—and left it by the Delhi Gate, where the walls are seventy feet high, and covered with parroquets, and near which are the comfortable-looking quarters of the married European troops. The officers have elegant and commodious-looking quarters in the centre of the ground, which is tastefully laid out, and strikes one as a most desirable abode.

Close to the charming Hall of Audience,

with its rich inlaid-work and transparent marble tracery, is the little mosque of Moti-Musjid, or the Pearl Mosque, a perfect gem of white marble with black lines, which bring into relief the exquisite work on the walls. How plain and grand it all is; how different from the ornaments of Roman Catholic cathedrals! This was built by no worshippers of images, but believers in the doctrine that there is one God.

On the city side of the open space which detaches the fort stands the Jama Masjid, the largest mosque in India, with two lofty minarets; one of which we ascended, and had a most magnificent view of Delhi and its neighbourhood. In and around that building in 1857 assembled 40,000 men to pray for success to the rebel armies, and there on Friday, 9th December, 1881, we saw two or three thousand Mussulman worshippers bowing in the direction of Mecca: not south-east, as we had seen them do before, but north-west, within sound of the British bugles and in the presence of a few wandering travellers, chiefly Scotch, come out to view this wondrous land.

A very handsome museum and literary institute has been erected at one end of the Queen's Gardens, and the railway terminus close by is one of the most conspicuous buildings in the city.

Our drive on Friday evening was of a very interesting and almost exciting character. The British Commissioner, Major Young, was good enough to accompany us; and explain in most graphic language, on the ground, the principal events of the siege and storming of Delhi by a handful of British and Sikh troops in 1857.

We first visited the Cashmere Gate; this and the ramparts on each side are left unrepaired, exactly in the same state as they were when Nicholson's forlorn hope saved the British Empire in Hindostan; then we ascended the famous "ridge" from which there is a view of the city, a good deal like that of Damascus from the mountain: to a certain extent commanding it, but separated from it by narrow gullies, which the mutineers made use of to annoy the British force. On the highest point has been erected a monumental pillar to the memory of the brave men who performed one of the most remarkable exploits in history. The inscription on its base tells a tale of valour which has never been excelled.

The whole besieging force amounted to 9,866, the casualties were 3,854; the 1st Bengal Fusiliers had 427 men before the city, of whom 319 were *hors de combat.*

"Delhi must be taken," wrote Sir John Lawrence, from the Punjaub. "The thing is impossible, we have not force to do it," was the commander's reply. What must have been the feelings of one of the most humane and tender-hearted of men, in the full knowledge of the terrible sacrifice of valuable life involved in his rejoinder, when that rejoinder was "*Delhi must be taken.*" He knew better than any man then living the attitude of the Sikhs, the magnitude of the crisis, and the absolute necessity of the fall of the ancient capital; and that reiterated order saved India to England, although it did not prevent the man who issued it being hooted by a London crowd, because he did not approve of the recent war in Afghanistan.

The population of Delhi was, and is yet, disarmed, because by no means well-affected to our rule; and consequently game abounds in all directions round the city. One would never imagine, looking down from the "ridge," that a great mosque, a red fort, two station towers, and a few low minarets rising among gardens, represented a city of 160,000 inhabitants.

The debateable land between the Cashmere Gate and the Memorial Tower is now covered with villas and wide avenues, and the Nicholson Gardens, overlooking the Jumna, occupy a considerable portion of it.

It was bitterly cold when at 8 o'clock on Saturday morning we drove out of the Ajmere Gate over a dusty plain covered with tombs, reminding one of the Roman Campagna and the Appian way. The modern Delhi is comparatively new; centuries ago there were cities on that flat.

Our destination was the Khotub Minar, the highest pillar in the world, 238 feet above the ruined Hindoo temples and Mahometan mosques at its base, and 860 years old. It is a wonderful and very imposing structure, of red sandstone outside, and inside of white granite. The ascent is laborious, and did not repay me, for one sees nothing but a dreary, tomb-covered, dusty plain. Here, as in many other places, we were mobbed by beggars; there is, indeed, dire poverty in this land; the squalor, emaciation and dirt are sometimes appalling.

We spent rather a dismal Sunday, two of our party being ill: principally in consequence of the miserable accommodation and cooking at the Northbrook Hotel. I was attracted by the name, and outside it looked well enough; but altogether it answered to the scriptural description of a whited sepulchre.

The hotels in India are hardly worthy of the name; few British travellers visit it, and they nearly all stay with the officials; ours is the first family party that ever went up country, and we of course have to pay in many little discomforts the usual penalty of pioneers of progress.

I write now in Clark's Hotel, at Lahore—a little whitewashed bungalow some distance outside the city, with one lofty stable-like public room in the centre, and half a dozen square vaults as bedrooms opening out of it, three at each side ; but here the landlady is an Englishwoman, the victuals are tolerable, and sanitary arrangements are well attended to.

We left Delhi at mid-day on Monday, 12th December, and were detained half an hour at Ghazeeabad Junction waiting for the Calcutta train. There is much sandy and sterile land in this neighbourhood, and we saw some large herds of deer, but as you approach Meerut city and cantonment the country improves. The stations are prettily adorned with convolvulus and other flowers, and all the short time we have been in India we have been struck everywhere with the good roads. Our friends at home have little idea how far behind they are in this respect, some of our leading lines of communication being simply disgraceful.

After a good dinner in the refreshment-room at Suharunpore, we made all snug for the night, and did not get up until within sight of the minarets of the famous mosque at Amritsir.

Passing close to the camp of Meean Meer, with its numerous tents and elephants, we reached the imposing fortress-looking station of Lahore at 8.30, and found waiting us two carriages sent by Lady Egerton, wife of the Governor, he himself being absent in camp. One of them was a lofty drag seated for ten and drawn by four camels, a postilion dressed in the bright scarlet of the paramount power riding on each.

In this singular vehicle, which sometimes attained the rate of ten miles an hour, we drove round the city after breakfast, through the Lawrence Gardens; there, joined to each other, are the Lawrence and Montgomery Halls; there is also a collection of wild animals; and in various directions past the college are seen courts of law, and other public buildings.

The British residents all live outside the city, in separate bungalows of more or less pretensions, and have their names written in large letters on the entrance-pillars. The European shopkeepers do the same. On the side of a wide avenue, beneath a spreading tree, you see an immense board announcing "Mrs. Reid, dressmaker."

We ascended one of the four minarets of the principal mosque, and obtained a really magnificent view of the city and its surroundings—the sandy wastes on either side of the river Ravee, the low, mean-looking houses within the walls, and the innumerable villa gardens without; and in the evening we were present at an amateur concert in the bungalow of Mr. Justice Elsmie, which was crowded with the beauty and fashion of Lahore. There are no fewer than 250 members of an English society here. We drove to it in our camel-carriage, drawn this time by only two camels, and had to pay forfeit for our barbaric splendour, as the creatures' heads were too high for the covered entrance-porch, and we had to get out in the dust.

Lahore has a population of nearly 100,000, and the extensive railway works employ 2,000 people. The Bishop (French), formerly a Church missionary, called upon us—an earnest, liberal-minded man, highly respected in northern India.

Here let me say that nothing so much impedes the progress of Christianity in that country as the proceedings of certain High Church dignitaries, who so thoroughly mistake the doctrines of our most holy faith, and misrepresent the teachings of their Divine Master, as to treat clergymen of other denominations as beyond the pale, and very much on a level with the heathen. Hindoo inquirers ask if it is not true that a certain bishop says that the difference between Presbyterians and Episcopalians is fundamental ; and that another bishop withdrew the licenses of twenty-three clergymen because they would not conform to his ritualistic practices. Everyone I meet deplores the mischief done by bigots of this kind.

The schools of the American Presbyterian Mission are said to be the most successful educational enterprise in the province. It cannot be for a moment doubted that, although the converts of the missionaries in Hindostan are few and far between, their teaching is shaking to its very centre the whole fabric of heathen mythology. The upper and educated classes have no belief in the gods of their fathers. I find in a hymn-book, composed by Lála Behári Lál for the use of an association of Hindoo reformers, the following, which might be sung in any Christian church:—

"Thou art my Maker;
Thou art the Creator of the World,
Thine's all the universe:
Blessed be Thy name.

"The sun and moon while turning
Speak forth Thy praise;
Thou weighest the earth in balances:
Blessed be Thy name.

"The wind as it blows
Opens the door to Thy glory,
And wafts abroad Thy divinity:
Blessed be Thy name.

"From the smallest tree,
From the ant to man,
All is created by Thee:
Blessed be Thy name.

"All the rivers and seas
Are full of Thy righteousness;
Thou art limitless, eternal;
Blessed be Thy name.

"Thy name is great
Who hath wrought all these works;
I offer all my praise to Thee:
Blessed be Thy name."

Lahore for many centuries has been the resort of learned men, and the native believers in one God have now their full complement there.

One of our visits was to the tomb of Runjeet Singh—of white marble with black lines—a conspicuous object on the wall below the Fort. Four wives and seven concubines were burnt at his burial. Another was to the Government prison, where 2,400 men are confined, 500 more being in another building some distance off, and a third containing 250 women. All the arrangements, as far as eating, houses, and cleanliness are concerned appear to be admirable, but one fresh from Europe does not like to hear the clanking of so many chains. They make the most beautiful carpets, and I ordered one, to be ready in six months, at a price which would rather surprise a British shopkeeper. A third visit was to the famous Shalamar Gardens, laid out in 1637 by the Emperor Shah Jehan. They consist of a great plantation of mango-trees, with many fountains and beds of roses, and are really very pretty and shady. I asked the custodian if he could show us the fruit of the mango. He said that these trees had borne none for two years; and when I inquired the reason, I received the truly Eastern answer—"God knows!"

Next morning we were very busy, and took full advantage of our camel-carriage. The day before Christmas an exhibition of all the manufactures and artistic productions of the Punjaub, for which a special building has been erected, was to be opened, and Mr. Kipling, Director of the School of Art, who had charge of it, kindly allowed us to have a private view. There were a great many beautiful things, and some of them marvellously cheap. We next visited the Museum, chiefly remarkable for a valuable collection of Græco-Bactrian Buddhist sculptures, from the Peshawur district. After that we went to the College, in which two institutes are combined under one roof, and Dr. Leitner, the enthusiastic Principal, showed us over the building. There are ninety-seven students in the English department, each of whom receives two rupees a month from the Government, and 192 in the Oriental classes, which are supported entirely by voluntary subscriptions. Dr. Leitner, who told us that he himself was supposed to speak twenty-five languages, has raised among the rich natives three lacs of rupees for this institution; and we had the great satisfaction of seeing and hearing students from all parts of Central Asia, in clean, airy class-rooms, being taught mathematics, chemistry, medicine, law—in fact, all the branches of an ordinary University education. They were of all ages, and most of them holy men—priests of their respective faiths. Think for a moment of the immense influence which such an institution as this must have in all the vast regions north as well as south of the Himalayas!

We devoted the afternoon to the inspection of the native town of Lahore—a strange admixture of fantastically carved and painted houses with mud hovels. In the rough, narrow, unpaved and almost impassable streets, are open bazaars, where both wares and vendors are covered with flies. In spite of a great deal of filth and squalor, singularly enough, there is an almost entire absence of bad smells. The Wazir and Golden Mosques are curious edifices, in the centre of the city.

These Punjaubees are a far finer and more stalwart race than the Hindoos, and some of the regiments in our service look very well indeed.

CHAPTER IV.

AGRA AND THE TAJ MAHAL.

WE left by the evening train on 15th December, and soon after I awoke next morning I descried a range of dark mountains on the left. Presently, as the sun got a little above the horizon, it shone upon what I first thought was a cloud; for a moment it did not occur to me that the sky was cloudless. I took up Stanford's admirable travelling map of India, and saw at once that the object was the summit of Kedarnath, or an adjoining peak, 22,900 feet high, and about 130 miles off.

My first sight of the Himalayas was not disappointing; and for two or three hours afterwards, every time I looked out of the window, there was that great white solemn mountain piercing the sky. There were a number of birds flying all about us that morning—kingfishers, kites, cranes, storks, ducks, the beautiful blue Indian jay, and many others unknown to me.

D 2

We spent twenty-four hours in the Empress Hotel, Meerut—a building in which twenty-one people, being all its occupants, were murdered in 1857. Here the Mutiny commenced, and I wanted to see it on that account; and also because it is one of the most important cantonments and military stations in India. Some of the bungalows are very large, especially those occupied by the King's Dragoon Guards; and the Mall is the broadest and best-made avenue in our Eastern possessions, or perhaps anywhere else.

Returning to Ghazabad, we proceeded on the East Indian Railway over a poorly-cultivated plain, where many herds of cattle, buffaloes, sheep, and goats, and occasionally deer, derived a very precarious subsistence from the burnt-up pasture; mango-orchards and cotton-fields occasionally relieved the landscape. It was nearly 9 o'clock when, tired, dusty, and thirsty, we found ourselves drinking champagne in Laurie and Staten's hotel—a large bungalow in the European quarter, which covers a great space of ground outside Agra Fort.

Next day was Sunday, and we mixed with a most picturesque-looking congregation of civilians and soldiers in the English church, where the Rev. Father O'Neill, a well-known High Church enthusiast and celibate, preached an impassioned sermon from the words, "The Lord is at hand."

After tiffin I had my first view of what most travellers believe to be the finest building in the world—the Taj Mahal—a mausoleum of pure white marble, built by Shah Jehan for his beautiful queen Moomtaza-Zumanee—the Light of the World—and in erecting which 20,000 men were employed for twenty-two years, at a cost of between two and three millions sterling. It is as white as when first built, and richly decorated with mosaics inlaid with jasper, agate, cornelian, and other precious stones, all the work of Italian artists some 250 years ago. The building itself stands on a marble terrace 400 feet square, with a minaret 100 feet high at each corner. Between it and the magnificent entrance-gate built of red sandstone and marble, is one of the most beautiful gardens that I have seen in the East.

At one end of the platform is a mosque in the same style and of the same materials as the gateway, and at the other end a building architecturally to match, but not consecrated as a place of worship.

I had expected great things, but found that I had formed no conception of the reality. Anything so fairy-like, so spotless, so gracefully gigantic, so totally unlike other creations of man, I did not imagine had existence on earth. I have now seen it from various points of view —from the gateway, from under the shade of the forest-trees in the garden, from a distance, from the top of one of the minarets, from the lofty platform overlooking the Jumna; and each time that I shut my eyes and opened them again it seemed like a heavenly vision, a something utterly superhuman dropped down by the celestials to astonish man. I now understand what a friend once said to me: "When you see the Taj at Agra, you will say it is worth while going to India for that sight alone." Photography, painting, and even sculpture fail to give one an adequate idea of this amazing tomb, and all the descriptions of it that I have ever read convey but the faintest notion of its perfect beauty.

Agra Fort is a lofty and imposing edifice of red sandstone, visible from a distance in all directions, and dominating both banks of the Jumna for miles around. Besides the British barracks, it contains the Palace of Akbar, with public and private reception-halls of white marble, resembling those at Delhi, and the Pearl Mosque, of the same material. How simple and grand it is — only lotus flowers carved on the walls, and a few tastefully-coloured mosaics: no tawdry images or ornaments disfigure the place. How suitable for the worship of Jehovah!

The largest mosque in Agra—the Jumma Musjid—is so close as almost to form a part of the railway-station, the whistles of the locomotives and the cry of the muezzins strangely mixing, and filling one's mind with thoughts of how this great Eastern problem is likely to be solved.

The streets of the native city are tolerably

wide and well paved. The bazaars are stocked with vast quantities of goods, and many elaborately-carved houses afford evidence of commercial prosperity. The traveller in the country cannot fail to be struck with the spacious and well-made roads intersecting the English quarter in the neighbourhood of every large town, and the obsequious respect shown to the sahibs driving in their carriages by the natives in bullock-carts or on foot.

The winter smell of India is not pleasant; the people, feeling the cold acutely, and being as a rule very poor, without the means of procuring proper fuel, burn all sorts of refuse, and everywhere the dull, sickening odour meets you, stealing into large bungalows and even permeating the cooking. The number of huge kites, brown and white, and of carrion crows, seems surprising; but then they are the scavengers of this land; no one thinks of molesting them, and well do they do their duty.

We have enjoyed many drives in the neighbourhood of Agra, and remark here, as elsewhere, the quantity and infinite variety of the birds. Every two or three yards we come upon minas in twos and threes, with dusky-red plumage, a little larger than a blackbird; then there are green bee-eaters, the same as in Egypt; hoopoes, blue jays of dazzling colours, and other flying creatures, large and small, the Hindu names of which would not be edifying.

The prettiest place near Agra is Sikandra—the tomb of Akbar, from which was taken the Koh-i-noor. It is situated in a large enclosure, laid out precisely like an English nobleman's park, the trees and flowering-shrubs in which are very beautiful, the stately tamarinds being especially conspicuous, on account of their height and spreading foliage. Then there is a lovely tomb in a garden on the other side of the Jumna, which you reach by a very rickety bridge of boats; it is that of Itmad-ud-daulah; a perfect gem of white marble inlaid with precious stones, the workmanship of which, and particularly the marble screens, fills one with astonishment.

The principal excursion is to Fattehpur-Sikri, which Akbar founded 250 years ago, and intended to make his capital; but he was forced to abandon it because of the badness of the water. It is twenty-three miles distant, but there is an excellent road; and it took us only three hours to drive to it. We met great numbers of carts, drawn by oxen, taking cotton and hewn stones and agricultural produce into the city, and passed through several miserable-looking villages of mud-hovels, closely resembling those in Upper Egypt.

The palace, and the mosque called Bhund-Darwaza, occupy a lofty eminence on a great plain. The gateway of the latter is probably the finest in India, and rises 130 feet above the plateau; the quadrangle is 433 by 336 feet, and inside of it there is a fairy-like vision, in the shape of a holy man's tomb, of the finest pierced work in white marble that I ever saw. It is just like lace; and you can scarcely realise the fact that these delicately-traced screens of large size are really carved out of one block of so hard a material.

When Akbar constructed this great edifice he was aspiring to be the chief imam of a reformed religion, and attempted in its quadrangle to expound his faith; but his courage failed; and all he could do was with stammering lips to repeat a stanza which one of his favourites had composed, which to my mind seems a good and orthodox sermon, and which may be translated thus:—

"The Lord to me the kingdom gave,
He made me good and wise and brave,
He guided me in faith and truth,
He filled my heart with right and ruth;
No wit of man can sum His state,
Allahu Akbar! God is great!"

We wandered for an hour among the silent ruins of his palace, saw an English class being taught in a room once belonging to the zenana, and were amused at being told that one tower, the divisions of which appeared to us very extraordinary, had been constructed so as to enable the emperor's ladies to play to the best advantage the game of blind-man's-buff. The buildings here, and in many other places we have visited, are being repaired and restored by the Government at great expense. It cannot be said that there is any neglect of the ancient monuments of India.

The principal grain on the fields at this time of year is pulse. There is a variety of other cereals used by the people, such as moong, urd, &c., and every second or third shop in the bazaars and villages is for the sale of provisions.

One day we were entertained to a performance by two female jugglers, and certainly some of the tricks are very remarkable; but that of the mango-tree appeared to us easily explicable. On two other occasions we drove through the bazaars of the city, which are extremely interesting, the costumes of buyers and sellers, the ladies in the balconies, and the monkeys on the roofs constituting a scene thoroughly Oriental. Then a couple of harpers used to come into the bungalow of an evening, and nothing could be funnier than their singing, in Hindu accents, "We won't go home till morning, till daylight does appear."

Mr. Lawrence, Deputy-Collector of the district, was kind enough to call and show me over the various offices under his control ; and also beneath the same roof I had the advantage of hearing trials, both of civil and criminal cases.

To-day I have seen two corpses being carried on men's shoulders to be cremated, carefully covered, but without coffin or funeral pall. Those of the richer natives are attended by many mourners, making a loud wailing noise, the bones and ashes being conveyed to the Ganges, as being holier than the Jumna, which is close at hand.

I have been four times to the Taj, and my original impression has not altered at all. The red sandstone of the adjacent buildings takes away from its effect, more especially at a distance; but the proportions, the colour, the workmanship and the design of the structure are perfectly lovely; you can scarcely realise, so admirable are the lines, that the dome is 247 feet above the garden.

My wife spent the forenoon of our last day in Agra in accompanying Miss Johnston, a lady from Forfarshire connected with the Medical Mission, on her visits to several of the zenanas of the poorer women of the city. Miss Johnston carried her medicine-chest with her, and administered to those who stood in need of her aid. These poor people have no means of getting medical advice, as no man, unless connected with the family, is allowed to visit them; and the best that can be done is for their husbands to tell their symptoms to a doctor. Some of the houses were very poor and extremely wretched, totally destitute of furniture, and the lives of their inmates appeared to my wife to be one of utter misery. The women received the medicines with the greatest gratitude. Surely this is the most potent lever that a missionary can use!

Mr. Thomson, Professor of English Literature in the University—an Arbroath man—called upon me in the morning; Dr. Valentine, the respected medical missionary, whom I have now seen twice, hails from Brechin; Mr. Weir, the banker from whom I got my money, told me that his father was a clergyman in Arbroath; and, to cap the Forfarshire connexion, when I asked the station-master to reserve a carriage for us for Lucknow, he told me that he would do so with great pleasure, and more especially as his name, although he was an Eurasian, was William Baxter, and his father came from Scotland!

CHAPTER V.

LUCKNOW AND CAWNPORE.

At 6.22 p.m., on 24th December, we left Agra; and, amidst the most frightful noise—shunting in various directions, and bumping of too severe a description to be consistent with a Christian state of mind—at Cawnpore Junction, about 3 o'clock in the morning, I heard the exclamation, "A merry Christmas to you!" Between 6 and 7 we were whirled off in gharries—the rough covered cabs of the country—from the station to Hill's "tumble-down-dick" Hotel in Lucknow; and I don't know why, but my first remark on entering it was, "We are now 7,000 miles from London."

No rain has fallen here since the first week in September, and the dust lies thick, not only on all the roads, and roofs, and walls, but on the topmost leaves of every tree. Most of the trees of India are evergreen, or nearly so; those which do not absolutely answer to this description only shedding their leaves for a week or two in February. Rain is very much wanted now, and I hear fears already expressed regarding the state of the crops.

People at home can scarcely realise what vast districts in India are every now and then on the brink of famine. Oude is one of the finest provinces in the country; yet a gentleman in high position told me that of its 11,000,000 inhabitants 4,000,000 were insufficiently fed, and double that number just able to get enough to sustain them, rendering anything like payment for education totally out of the question.

I went on Sunday morning to the American Methodist Episcopal Church, where one of the missionaries delivered a very striking and original discourse appropriate to the season. Some of our party went to a church which shall be nameless, where the clergyman delivered no discourse at all, but simply told a large congregation of high-bred British ladies and gentlemen not to get drunk at Christmas-time!

Lucknow, the City of Roses, is quite a modern

place—only 100 years old—but has a population of nearly 300,000. It may be styled, like Washington, the city of magnificent distances, so widely spread are the European dwellings all around it. Its two chief characteristics are the number of gaudy, gingerbread-looking, painted stucco palaces and temples, the tawdry tinsel of which makes one feel quite angry (more particularly after seeing Agra), and the remarkable beauty of its public gardens and parks. I don't know any city so highly favoured in this respect. The Wingfield Park is unsurpassed for the variety of its forest trees; and nothing can exceed the loveliness of the flowers, the flowering shrubs, the walks and beds in the Residency, which has been left in ruins, just as it was when the mutineers marched out of it, after the rescue and retreat of that band of heroes whose exploits astonished the world. I have examined the ground with the greatest care; have stood uncovered at Sir Henry Lawrence's grave; have been twice in early morning to the neighbouring gate of the city where General Neil was shot; and to me it is simply

RESIDENCY GARDEN AT LUCKNOW.

inconceivable how the original 600 could have held out for a day against 60,000 assailants with upwards of 300 pieces of cannon. I have climbed to the top of one of the lofty minarets of the mosque adjoining the Imambarra Palace; I have ascended to the top of the Martinière College, on an eminence overlooking the city; and how Sir Henry Havelock, and then Sir Colin Campbell, managed, with a handful of men, first to relieve the Residency, and then to take the city by storm, passes my comprehension. No more striking instances exist in history of what British soldiers can do when led by competent men.

The tale of the siege of Lucknow appeared to me a marvellous one at the time; now that I have trod the ground, it seems something like a miracle, and one cannot help remarking what a fine, determined-looking body of men inhabit this capital of Oude. Its fantastic domes and minarets look far better in photographs than in the reality; just think of these yellow and pink coloured arches of plaster and paint after the glorious Taj! "'Tis distance lends enchantment to the view." I get away from them as fast as possible, to wander among the poinsettia, bougainvilleas, hibiscus and oleander of the gardens; and the banians, peepuls, and tamarinds of the Park.

The bazaars are extremely amusing. I find it impossible to describe them, but can only refer to an illustrated copy of "The Arabian Nights."

A very interesting drive is to the Alumbagh, the scene of so much fighting in those terrible times. On our way we passed the camp of the commissariat elephants—a novel spectacle to a European.

On the forenoon of the 27th December, there was a gathering of the school-children of the American Mission in the Wingfield Park, for the distribution of Christmas prizes. It was addressed by the Rev. Mr. Johnson, from Shahjehanpore, and the Rev. Mr. Parker from Moradabad, both of whom spoke with the utmost fluency in Hindostani, and seemed to rivet the attention of the audience; and I was unexpectedly called upon to make a speech in the centre of India, just a month after I had landed on its shores. Then we lunched with Colonel Worsley, with whom I examined some of the expensive new barracks in process of erection; and we heard the band of the 7th Native Infantry play admirably in the Wingfield Park in the evening.

The extraordinary sounds one hears at night outside these bungalows in the neighbourhood of Indian towns are surprising. There are dogs and wild beasts of various descriptions, but louder than all, the yelling of the men who are hired to keep them off the compounds, and also to protect the houses against thieves. They mostly belong to predatory bands themselves, and in this manner levy a sort of black-mail on the inhabitants. "There is no stillness in Indian life," said an officer's wife to me to-day. Her husband a few hours before had remarked, while we were plodding through the dust under a fiery, burning sun, "This is our cold weather!"

At daylight on Wednesday morning, 28th December, we were galloping in gharries full speed to the railway station—why they should go at this furious pace, *quien sabe?* The Oude and Rohilcund Railway Company provided us with the most spacious and well-constructed carriage that I have seen in India, in which we travelled over a fertile and well-wooded plain back to Cawnpore. These Indian plains are endless, unbroken; there is no undulation, or hillock, or mound of any kind to relieve their vast monotony.

The train slackens its speed—a great viaduct is before us, and we get our first sight of the sacred Ganges. At this season it is not a very imposing river, but the wide expanse of sand shows what a mighty stream it must be after the rains.

Sergeant Lee, a very remarkable man, now keeps the clean little railway hotel—a bungalow near the station. He went out to India in 1844, has marched from Peshawur to Calcutta, 2,200 miles in four months, was in nearly all the great battles in Scinde; marched to the relief of Lucknow and Cawnpore, with Sir Henry Havelock and Lord Clyde; although three times wounded has enjoyed perfect health,

MASSACRE GHAUT AT CAWNPORE.

without ever being home, or even up to the hills; is very well to do, and very thankful to God for his position and success in life.

I write at the close of a memorable day, when, under his guidance, and listening to his vivid and naturally eloquent descriptions, we have visited the scenes of the awful catastrophe —the three wells: first, that into which were thrown the bodies of those who died in Wheeler's entrenchment, and for which no cemetery could be found among the living; the second, from which the besieged could alone draw water, always at the peril of their lives, as it was commanded by the enemy's guns; the third, into which were heaped the mutilated bodies of Nana Sahib's victims, which now stands in the midst of a most beautiful garden, and over which has been erected a memorial screen, and a statue by Baron Marochetti. We sat on the steps of the ghaut where the too-confiding ones embarked, and were fired upon; inspected the monuments in the handsome Memorial Church; and for four hours listened to descriptions of horrors almost too terrible for relation.

It may be that the tale of the massacre, and what happened afterwards, may never be told. Things could be written about Sepoy barbarities in the next generation which could scarcely, having regard to the feelings of sorrowing families, be committed to paper while any of the victims are alive; and it may turn out that blowing from the guns was one of the mildest forms of retribution practised by the British troops.

The Mahommedans in Cawnpore are wealthy and influential; they raised large sums of money for the Turks during the Russian war, and nearly all are Jingoes, although notoriously disaffected to British rule.

CHAPTER VI.

ALLAHABAD AND BENARES.

WE left at mid-day for Allahabad, passing through the most fertile and best cultivated district we have seen in India—luxuriant crops, or their remains, of Indian corn, wheat, millet, pulse, and castor-oil, alternating with mango orchards and clumps of stately forest trees; lovely birds, conspicuous among which were the blue jay, the Sarus crane, and a kind of shrike with an orange breast, appearing in almost every field and grove. The day, as many of our days at this time were, was perfect, just like the finest in an English June; but several things reminded us that we were not at home—for example, jackals looking at us from the edge of the maize plantations.

At 5 o'clock wide roads, barracks, and other marks of a capital showed us that we were approaching Allahabad, "the City of God," which the railways have made a place of great importance. It is situated at the junction of the Ganges and the Jumna, and has a native population of upwards of a hundred thousand in addition to the Europeans, who muster strongly there, and whose bungalows, far apart, are separated from the crowded bazaars and streets of the city by the railway line. There are in the British quarter of Allahabad no fewer than ninety-seven miles of fine avenues, shaded by trees and well watered; and one morning I measured the breadth of a fair sample of them—Thornhill Road—and found it to be fifty-five paces.

Chief Justice Sir Robert Stuart and his lady were in the railway-station waiting for us, and I do not recollect in any part of the world having been treated with more overflowing hospitality. Some of us lived in his bungalow, and he insisted upon the whole party dining there every day, where we met many of the leading residents, and altogether had what the Americans call "a right good time of it;" military men, civilians, and journalists contributing to add to our stock of knowledge of Indian affairs.

The day after our arrival Mr. Douglas

Straight, who sat in the House of Commons with me for four years, and who is now one of the Justices of the North-west Province, drove us to the picturesquely-situated fort at the confluence of the rivers, where thousands of devotees were washing in the sacred waters. We had a fine view from the ramparts, but the sun was very hot; and we were glad to escape from it to inspect one of those casemates where everything is kept in readiness, in the event of any attack being made upon one of the most important positions in India.

In the evening Mr. Straight and other friends provided myself and my daughters with horses, and we rode among the fashionables in Alfred Park. Near that tastefully laid out pleasure-ground is the Mayo Hall, from the top of whose tower I had a fine view of the city and neighbourhood, and in which one evening there was a ball that I attended. The Muir College, in process of building, named after a former respected and popular governor of the province, is also near the Park.

I visited likewise the Christian village

founded by Sir William and Lady Muir, between the European quarter and the Ganges; and was shown over the church, school, and clean native houses by the pastor, Rev. Mr. Mohen, who speaks English very well, and was glad to see a party of strangers.

The variety of costumes, vehicles, and wares, the cries, the curious groups of creatures clothed and unclothed, the scenes which one beholds every moment in the streets and bazaars of Allahabad, are so totally different from everything an untravelled Briton ever saw, or could imagine, that description would certainly be in vain.

I get up every morning and walk in the Chief Justice's garden, examining the fruits and flowers —what a magnificent display of roses!—and rejoicing in the thought that an unclouded sun appears every day, and that no rains or storms can interfere with our plans of travel. There are no bells in Indian houses, nor do native servants wear shoes or stockings; when anything is wanted, the master or mistress calls "Qui hai!" and instantly from some obscure corner an unnoticed menial noiselessly appears.

I went on Sunday morning with Lady Stuart to service in the English Church, which was extremely well conducted ; but the sermon —not by the minister himself—consisted of a dozen sentences, although it was New Year's day ; and surely something might have been said, of a solemn and impressive nature, suited to the occasion.

Shortly after 8 o'clock on the following morning we were again in our railway-carriage, and crossing the great bridge over the Jumna passed for a long distance through a rich and well-wooded country, where there were many fields of flax in addition to the usual crops. One is struck by the immense distances over which these railways are carried in absolutely straight lines, a curve being quite a novelty. To-day we have made the fastest run which we have yet had in this country—viz., from Sirsia to Mirzapore : 32 miles in an hour. The gauge of most of the Indian railways is midway between that of the North Western and the Great Western, or almost, if not exactly, the same as that originally laid down between Dundee and Arbroath.

There are a good many miles of a poor, sandy country; and, what is a novelty in these unbroken plains, a few hills before arriving at Mogul-Serai, which is the junction for Benares, situated six miles off the main line.

We were all disappointed with the first view of this place, the holy city of the Hindoos, whose 200,000 inhabitants are crammed into a very small space on a bluff on the left bank of the Ganges, and whose beauties have been a good deal exaggerated both by pen and pencil. Clark's Hotel, fully three miles from the railway station, is said to be the best in India; and certainly its landlady—a native, and not even of high caste, although married to an Englishman—does everything in her power, and successfully, to make it so.

The Maharajah of Benares sent two open carriages to the railway-station for us, and placed them at our disposal during our residence. He is now simply a great nobleman, or zemindar, having an income of thirteen lacs of rupees; and as he was at his country house, some distance from the city, a gentleman of eminence, and much in his confidence, Mr. Shivpershad, called upon us, and offered his services. He was brought up in the Education Department, and has lately had the honour of being elected a member of the Supreme Council of India; speaks English not only fluently but elegantly; ridicules the idea of any danger to this great country from Russia; strongly deprecates the policy which culminated in the Afghan War, and maintains that the principal thing that India and its people ardently desire is peace. He took us first to visit the College, where there are 1,000 students; then to the Town Hall, the gift of a munificent native; and afterwards through the chief and very crowded street of the city to a temple inhabited by a vast number of monkeys.

A great deal of money is spent in Benares, as rich people come from all parts of the Hindoo world, a few years before they expect their end, in order to die in the holy city. The fluctuations of commerce and the introduction of railways have led in India, as in other countries, to many ups and downs in the fortunes of cities.

Since Allahabad has become a great junction, Mirzapore, its once flourishing rival, has dwindled away; but the sacred Benares will always hold its own as long as the Hindoo religion lasts.

There are very few converts to Christianity in this part of Hindostan. "Very, very slowly," said a missionary of the London Society to me the other day, "does the work go on;" but then he showed me a High School, where he and one of his European colleagues, assisted by twenty-four natives, teach 500 boys, imparting religious as well as secular instruction; and he told me that not only is the number of pilgrims steadily falling off, but that their contributions for purposes of their faith have likewise so much declined that the Punga, or principal priest of one of the temples, was lately obliged to mortgage the whole of its property in order to pay expenses.

Some of our friends, it appears to me, attach far too much importance to making open and avowed converts to Christianity. They forget how many people there may be—women, for example—in this land who, if they changed their nominal religion would lose their caste, and their husbands too. May they not be excused for being Christians in secret, and thus not becoming chargeable to the funds of some society, which they certainly otherwise would do? The converts, no doubt, are few; but the sapping and mining process is going on all the time. The civilians who oppose the missionaries, but who, in fact, know very little about them, admit this to be the case. There is among the masses a cessation of hostility to Christian instruction—completely in some parts of the country, and more or less so in all; and although the attitude of the higher class of natives who have abandoned belief in Hindooism is not hopeful, as far as Christianity is concerned, the lower classes have not become Deists, like their betters; and the known want of faith of the latter is beginning to be felt as an important factor in the feeling of the Indian peasantry towards the religion of their governors.

There are said to be 5,000 temples and 350 mosques at Benares. One of the former is tenanted solely by monkeys, which also swarm in the city generally, and their depredations are a serious source of loss to the inhabitants; so much so, that the municipality recently offered a reward for catching them, and taking them away to the jungle; but in vain. The creatures confine themselves almost entirely to the roofs of the houses, decline to be made prisoners, and, as no Hindoo would kill or injure them, are masters of the situation. Heaven forbid that I should ever again enter the Golden Temple and the various other sacred shrines in the centre of crowded Benares; the filth and odours from wretched specimens of humanity, fakirs and beggars, sacred bulls and monkeys, being simply indescribable! Even the beautiful gold brocade-work in the bazaars would hardly tempt me to enter those pestiferous narrow lanes.

Nothing can be more disappointing than the land side of this holy city. Secrole itself, which is the name of the European quarter, is much less inviting and pleasantly laid out than any of the other similar settlements which I have seen in the neighbourhood of Indian cities; but

Benares from the river in early morning is another thing altogether—a scene, a sight, a kind of dream never to be forgotten.

We drove in the Maharajah's carriages, attended by his intelligent Secretary, to a temple at a point just above the town ; and there embarked in his highness's state barge, manned by a crew of twelve in scarlet liveries, an official with a gigantic silver stick receiving us at the gangway. Amidships the vessel was covered with a gorgeous canopy, and from the prow projected two rampant wooden horses. Thus luxuriously did we drop down the sacred river for the whole length of the city, and nothing could exceed the picturesque effect produced by the rays of the just-risen sun upon its towers and domes and temples and palaces. The ghâts, or long flights of stone steps from the houses and streets to the stream, were crowded with devotees of both sexes and all ages, in every stage of nudity, yet modest withal, who were bathing in its holy waters, and filling from it their brightly-burnished brazen vessels. The priests were tinkling their cymbals of brass, and raising their voices aloud in praise of their gods; garments of the brightest hue glistened in the sun; fakirs held aloft their hands in adoration; and barges landed piles of wood, to burn the corpses laid on the banks; while goats, cows, donkeys, monkeys, vultures, parroquets and crows mingled freely with the devout multitude.

The architecture of some of the houses belonging to native princes strikes one every now and then as singularly chaste and effective; but adjacent mud hovels spoil the *coup d'œil.* Many of the ghâts are tumbling down, and the holy river is inexpressibly dirty. Just below the rough, rickety bridge of boats is the commanding site of the old fort, where also stood the city of Kasi, founded 1600 B.C. They are about to begin a great railway-bridge over the Ganges at this spot.

In the afternoon we witnessed another performance of jugglers, whose most remarkable trick was instigating a mongoose to kill a snake, whose head was reduced to pulp, but which, under the influence of their incantations, was restored to perfect health in a few minutes. Then they had scarcely gone when the verandah of the bungalow was covered with fruits and vegetables and native dishes presented to us by the Maharajah; and in the evening we had a delightful drive through mango-orchards, fields of barley in ear, springing wheat, beans, and vegetables of various kinds to the ruins of Sarnath, where Buddha himself once lived, and where he founded a religion even now professed by a great majority of the population of Asia.

There is a large business carried on in Benares in brass-work. Mrs. Clark, of the hotel, employs sixty people; and as scarcely any travellers require accommodation in India except in the cold season, the trade in brass is larger and more lucrative than that of keeping an inn.

On Thursday we enjoyed a remarkable and truly Oriental excursion to the Maharajah's castle of Ramnuggur, situated on a lofty bank several miles above and on the opposite side of the river from Benares, and commanding a strikingly-beautiful view of the city and its surroundings. First, we drove through gardens and fields of corn, then were carried in tangans —a sort of bath-chair, borne on poles by four coolies — to a sand-bank out in the stream, where the *Racehorse* barge was waiting to take us across to the picturesque stronghold, the battlements of which were manned by natives in all kinds of costumes and colours; while on the banks were carriages and caparisoned elephants, and troops of servants waiting to do our bidding—the great man is said to have no fewer than 3,000 retainers. He himself was at a distant country seat, but we were received by his nephew and heir, who showed us over the castle, introduced us to his little boy, who was learning English, let us see a performance by Nautch girls, and came, after we had lunched with friends in a pavilion in the beautiful gardens, to exhibit his horsemanship and his skill as a marksman by hitting à rupee thrown into the air with a rifle-ball—a feat which our entertainer, Mr. Ross, himself one of the best shots in India, and a member of a family celebrated for their prowess in this respect, said he could not perform. Then there were snake-charmers and actors from the Deccan, who played on the platform of the immense tank adjoining the garden.

We dropped down the river to the city at sunset in the barge, and in the evening attended a concert in aid of an asylum for widows, got up by Mr. Lambert, of the London Missionary Society, and patronised by all the officials. The jackals had a horrible chorus that night, and we were awakened at dawn by the trumpeting of elephants.

CHAPTER VII.

AT CALCUTTA.

ON the 6th of January, at mid-day, we joined the mail-train at Mogul-Serai Junction, and travelled over a vast, apparently interminable plain, well wooded and cultivated, fertile and irrigated; crossed the Sone at 4 o'clock on a great viaduct; halted fifteen minutes at the important military cantonment of Dinapoor; passed the city of Patna; at Mokameh had the best railway dinner we had tasted in India; at dusk found ourselves between strangely-shaped and isolated hills, and had hardly time to rub our eyes and tie up our wraps in the morning when, punctual to the moment, at 5·40 the train drew up in Howrah Station, on the other side of the Hooghly from Calcutta. The Government House drag, with four horses and two postillions, and various servants of the Viceroy, were waiting for us, and we were very soon comfortably installed in much more spacious apartments than we had occupied for some time.

I had a busy day, calling on merchants, missionaries, and other friends, and making various arrangements for our journey.

On Sunday morning I attended divine service at Union Chapel, in the Dhurumtollah, one of the most important streets in Calcutta; and immediately afterwards proceeded up the river in the Viceroy's steam-launch *Gemini*, to lunch with Lord and Lady Ripon at Barrackpore, where they generally spend Saturday and Sunday, in a villa situated in one of the most beautiful parks in all India. Opposite to it are the famous Baptist Mission premises of Serampore, identified with the names of Carey and Marshman, and where, being then Danish terri-territory, the early preachers of Christianity took refuge, when expelled by the Directors of the Company from British soil.

It was a beautiful sail, the scenery on both banks being very varied, and the foliage strikingly green even in winter. There were peepul, and tamarind, and palm-trees, picturesque-looking temples, great jute factories, with pretty villas attached ; boats of every sort and description, many of them like Venetian gondolas, passed up and down the stream; and brilliant flowers from overhanging gardens added colour to the landscape. The ever-greenness of Indian trees is one of the most striking features of the country; and I recollected when walking up the avenue of poinsettias and bamboos, which leads from the river-bank to the Viceregal country seat, that I had not seen rain, and hardly clouds, since we were in Munich, more than two months ago.

I was very glad to have a long conversation with the Marquis of Ripon: with whom I had been associated in the House of Commons in early life, and whose praises as a man and as a ruler I had heard with no surprise from persons of all political opinions and religious creeds wherever we had been during our Indian tour. I had expected, in consequence of the great change of policy since the Afghan war, to have found a good deal of difference of opinion with regard to Lord Ripon, but on the contrary there seemed to be none; everyone I met extolled his government, except an agent of some tea plantations, who knew as little about Indian politics as he did about the inhabitants of Jupiter.

Calcutta is a wonderful place, containing about 800,000 inhabitants, and the shipping of the Hooghly—vast steamers and sailing vessels from all parts of the world—gives one an exalted idea of its commercial importance. The Maidan, an immense open space larger than Hyde Park, immediately joins the river, and you have the unique sight of fashionable equipages dashing past within stone's-throw of Oceanic steamers.

We were a party of thirty at dinner at Government House on Monday evening, and I was happy to see Lord Ripon, after his recent severe illness, looking better than he has ever done in his life.

On Wednesday I had a very interesting excursion to the jute factory of Samnuggur, twenty-three miles up the river, where there are 4,000 workpeople and 415 looms. Mr. Smith, the manager, took us up in his steam-launch, and we were accompanied by Lord Lawrence, at present staying at Government House. We were extremely amused by the grinning countenances of the little boys employed: I never saw anything as good in a pantomime. The Hindoos learn to work very quickly; they will pick up as much in a week or ten days as a European will in six months, but are not very easily managed; and some of the factories on the river have never been able to get a sufficient number of hands, although the pay is excellent—two to three rupees a week; which in this country, especially when several members of the same family are employed, means affluence. Mr. Smith hospitably entertained us in his pretty bungalow on the river bank, and we sat in the verandah afterwards, watching the stream and the great jungle of bamboos opposite.

There was a children's fancy ball at Government House in the evening, and a picturesque sight it was: two hundred seniors appearing in costume, in addition to the young people and those living in the mansion.

Next morning I attended a meeting of the Legislative Council, in that famous chamber where so many resolutions for good and bad have been passed. Portraits of the various Viceroys hang on the walls, the evil countenance of Warren Hastings being the most conspicuous.

Even in the dead of winter the heat of the business portion of Calcutta oppresses me. I feel wearied driving in a gharry; and the crowds in the streets, on the stairs, and in the offices themselves, seem as if they would run you over. The jackals are as noisy in the early part of the night round Government House as we have heard them anywhere else. They live in the clumps of palms in the garden, and like the innumerable kites are never destroyed, as they are nature's best scavengers. The streets of Calcutta are wider than those of most Indian cities, tramways are used extensively, very handsome new public offices are in course of construction in Dalhousie Square, and the stranger will be struck with the bustle and activity everywhere visible.

I spent Friday morning with Major Baring, conversing principally on the financial condition of the country; and then inspected the very fine building occupied by the Bank of Bengal, where 300 clerks are employed.

It appears to me that India is likely now to take a step in advance; education, railways, newspapers and other influences are lifting it up as it were, breaking down old prejudices, letting in the light, and removing some of those causes which have hitherto had such a depressing effect on the population. The principal desideratum is a policy of peace, which will enable the Government to provide out of surplus revenue—first for the relief of the miserable masses from such taxes as that on salt, which bears so heavily on the poor; and then for the development of vast districts of the country, as yet neglected, by means of railroads and otherwise, so as to increase production, and avert famines. Such beneficial measures are out of the question if millions are to be thrown away on absolutely unnecessary and unjust frontier wars—wars which make enemies of proud neighbouring races, and which cost India infinitely more than the mere actual expenditure shown in the military accounts. It will be impossible largely to extend education, to open up communications, to provide the requisite irrigation, or to do many other things absolutely necessary for the future well-being of the people, unless there is an end to this system of picking quarrels for which they have got to pay. The natives with whom I have conversed, Hindoo and Mahometan as well, feel strongly on this point.

The recent endeavours of the Government to stimulate private enterprise, especially in the construction of railroads, instead of making them itself, are theoretically, and from a politico-economic point of view, quite right; but I doubt very much whether it will be possible, for a considerable time to come, to get much done in this way, unless the State is prepared to grant a guarantee, say, for a limited period of years; and I should be surprised were the able and judicious men now at the head of affairs here to insist too strongly on Government refusing all aid.

With respect to taxation in general, we at home must never forget that great consideration should be paid to the prevailing sentiment among educated natives, although it may appear to us founded on erroneous principles. On this point let me quote a few words from the *Indian Spectator*, a well-conducted newspaper published in Bombay :—" One important fact seems often to be forgotten by our rulers : that the views, opinions, and systems of free civilised countries of Europe, however good from the point of European politics and European economy, are not exactly or even approximately the views, opinions, and systems which ought to be circulated or enforced in a semi-civilised Asiatic country. It is needless at this time of the day to remind the authorities how vastly different are the political, social, and even economic conditions of this country from others. It has been more than once stated in these columns how dangerous it is to govern India on European principles." These cautions must be kept in mind in dealing with such matters as the tariff, the opium revenue, and the income-tax.

As far as I can learn, the question of the employment of natives in official life is making fair and satisfactory progress. I find no disposition whatever to discourage it on the part of those in power. One difficulty standing in the way of its more rapid extension is, that most of the better-educated classes amongst them are zemindars, or rich landed proprietors, whose interests are considered by the masses of the cultivators to be antagonistic to their own; so much so indeed that the latter are accustomed to look in preference to Europeans for justice.

CHAPTER VIII.

THE TEA-PLANTATIONS, DARJEELING.

THERE is an excellent custom at Government House, in Calcutta, of presenting each person living in the house with a printed list of the guests to be present at the dinner parties, so that you know whom you are to meet; and I thought that this might be very well imitated at some of the London entertainments.

We left for an excursion in the Himalayas on Saturday, 7th January, and were driven to the Sealdah Railway Station in the Viceregal chariot with the postillions. The scenery for many miles was more Oriental, as far as foliage was concerned, than any we had yet seen in India: dense jungle of bamboo alternating with gardens of palms, bananas, and mangoes, with occasional patches of wheat and tobacco; then came wide plains, with immense numbers of cattle and buffaloes feeding on almost invisible stubble; rows of fine tamarind-trees; picturesque houses of bamboo and mats, like representations of scenes in Borneo. At dark we reached the Ganges, crossing it in a steamer and dining on board.

I made myself comfortable for the night soon after entering the narrow-gauge railway on the other side, fell asleep shortly after 9 o'clock, and was astonished when a man shouted in my ear at 6 a.m., "next station Siliguri." Here we breakfasted, and took our seats in perhaps the most extraordinary and toy-like tram railroad which exists on the face of the earth. An American said of it the other day to a friend of mine: "I guess I have seen a good many queer things in the shape of railroads in my country, but this is the cheekiest little concern that ever I came across." The rails are two feet apart; the carriages are like low tram-cars; and so steep is the gradient—often 1 in 17—that little boys, seated on the engine, jump off at places where the sun has not melted the dew, to put sand on the rails, the tiny engine meantime puffing and blowing until the wheels can get a grip. At one place there is an actual loop, the train passing over a bridge which it had passed under a few minutes before.

I am one of those unfortunate people who become easily giddy looking down from great heights, and my friends had prepared me for a terrible experience on this line; but except at four or five unprotected curves close to Darjeeling, it was not nearly so bad as I had expected it would be. In many of the most dangerous places there is a substantial parapet, and trees and shrubs cover the sides of the steep hills, so that you are not sensible of the sheer precipice.

The views from time to time over mountains, hills, and valleys strike one with wonder; and we had not left Siliguri Station more than ten minutes when the white peak of Kinchinjunga appeared over the lofty neighbouring mountains like an aërial sentinel. Passing between tea-gardens, with their white, myrtle-like flowers, and by many cotton-trees, the striking red blossom of which yields a coarse material which the natives use, we soon reached real jungle, and now remarked the wonderful change which has come over the features of the people—we seemed all at once to have got among Kalmucks.

It would amuse a London-and-North-Western man to see the miserable hut which serves as the first station-house on the Darjeeling-Himalaya line. At this point it begins rapidly to ascend through a forest of exceeding beauty, many of the trees being very lofty, some of them having a canopy of flowers, and others covered with creepers of strange and weird-like shapes. There is a cart-track alongside the train-line, and every now and then you come upon stations to permit of conveyances passing each other, like those on the Suez Canal. There are a good many villages and shanties for the workmen who are employed in great numbers in repairing and altering the line. Occasionally you steam through a crowded bazaar, and the curves well merit the American's description.

Khersiong, surrounded on all hands by tea-gardens, is a bustling place; and we found the bazaars crowded by men, women and children of all the multifarious races which inhabit this part of Central Asia. The main street is only a few feet wide; but the steam-car puffs along the centre of it; and it would be difficult for a person who has never been out of Europe to imagine the scene at the market-place when we started after breakfast.

Nepaul, Thibet, Sikkim and Bhotan were all within sight from points on these lofty elevations; and hundreds of the races which dwell there are to be found employed on the railway, or on those great plantations of tea which are accomplishing almost a revolution in this remote portion of British territory.

Our engine had to stop several times, in consequence of bad coal, and it was nearly 6 o'clock in the evening when we arrived at Meadow Bank, one of Mr. Doyle's hotel-bungalows, which he had opened expressly for our large party, it having been shut for the cold months, as that was not the season in Darjeeling. Unfortunately the weather had become cloudy at mid-day, and we arrived in a kind of mist, auguring ill for a sight of the snowy ranges on the morrow.

We were up, however, betimes. At 6 a.m. the authorities pronounced the expedition to the hill from which the view is best seen undesirable; but at 7 o'clock there was a lift in the rolling clouds, the ponies were at the door, and I resolved to ride at least as far as the cantonment of Jellahbahar; the Commandant of which, Colonel Roberts, had kindly come down the evening before and offered to accompany us in the morning. About half-way up the acclivity which leads to his station I turned round on my saddle, and there, far up in the heavens, dense masses of clouds below them, were the Himalayan peaks, which I had so often longed to see. There was a time of comparative darkness again when we stopped at the Colonel's bungalow; but he, who had been asked to take care of us by Lieutenant-Colonel Kinloch, Younger, of Logie, and who showed us every attention during our stay at Darjeeling, was cheery and willing to do anything we wanted, and did not discourage my determination to go on at all hazards. So we descended to the tram-line at the first station, and then put our horses to face the steep path which conducts to the top of Senchal, 8,163 feet high, on which appeared conspicuously many lofty chimneys of deserted barracks, looking like ancient monuments. The barracks were condemned by the Public Works—or, as they call it in India, the Public Waste—Department, because the chimneys were unsafe, and they alone remain to tell the tale.

This is the highest point which travellers usually reach; but the Colonel shook his head when I asked if you really saw from it Mount Everest, the loftiest mountain in the world. "Tiger Hill," he said, "is the place," pointing to a wooded eminence 350 feet higher. "Then up we go," I replied, and in a very short time we were at the cairn on its summit, in the presence of a prospect which I confess fairly took away my breath.

Nothing that I had ever seen made me feel such a sense of awe. The clouds had passed away from that amazing Kinchinjunga group, and there stood revealed, apparently quite near, but really forty-five miles off, the stupendous mountain, 28,156 feet high. On its right, looking towards us, first Kabru, 24,015, and then the sloping peak of Junnu, 25,311. On the other side of the towering giant rose Pandim, 22,017, Narsing, 19,146, and the loveliest of all, a sugar-loaf of dazzling unbroken whiteness, 22,581, for which the surveyors have not yet found a name but which appears on the maps as "D. 2." We stood there for an hour rapt in admiration. Never before had I seen such a sublime prospect, and never can I hope to see such an one again. There are many views of the Alps, especially of the Bernese Oberland, which are more beautiful, perhaps more varied, but in point of immensity they are not for a moment to be compared to this. We were standing on the top of a hill twice the height of Ben Nevis, and facing a mountain seven times higher than the highest in Scotland. There was something almost un-earthly about it; I felt a kind of creeping cold-ness, and could hardly persuade myself that these towers and pinnacles were part of the earth on which we dwell. Then far away in the east were more vast mountains, capped by

Donkia, 23,187, the highest peak in Bhotan; and in the other direction the clouds kindly favoured us by lifting two or three times, and giving us glimpses of the summit of Mount Everest, 130 miles off. It was a day in my life never to be forgotten; the furthest point in our journey, the accomplishment of a desire long secretly cherished. I had seen the highest of the Himalayas in all their grandeur, and I knew that there was no prospect in the universe so magnificent as that of Kinchinjunga's snowy range from the point on which I stood.

There was hoar-frost every morning during our stay at Darjeeling, and although the sun was powerful at mid-day, we required all our warm clothing and wraps. The scenery on the mountain sides a good deal resembles that at Mentone and Monte Generoso, but on a far more stupendous scale—that is, the declivities are four or five times higher, while the lofty trees unknown to Europe, and graceful bamboos, constantly remind you that you are in Asia. At almost every turn you find houses and branches of trees covered with little flags of white and red paper and calico; these are Buddhist prayers, and the inscription on one and all of them is the same—four words of doubtful interpretation being repeated over and over again. I thought how striking an illustration this was of the words, "Use not vain repetitions as the heathen do."

We visited a celebrated Buddhist temple, and saw the circular praying-machines at work; it was but a better kind of hut after all, considerably adorned, and not so dirty as the Hindoo temples. Then we walked round the summit of the hill on which most of the bungalows stand under great banks of foliage—magnificent tree-ferns in hundreds—and were struck with the number of tall stately trees which had creepers almost to the top; the great Pothos parasite, several specimens of which we saw, never fails to kill its victim in the end. Rounding the western extremity of the hill, we obtained the best view of the settlement from what is called Edgar's Folly; why, I really don't know, because there is no point from which you could command so well the whole of Darjeeling. There are no roads for driving in this hill station; you must ride on a pony, or be carried on a dandy—a kind of couch on poles.

The people here complain very much of the Chinese resident ministers at the various Courts in Central Asia using their influence, and successfully, to keep the trade of all these countries in the hands of their own nation, and to prevent any extension of commerce with British India. Every one seems to have an interest of some kind or another in those tea plantations which are rapidly covering the hill-sides of that portion of Sikkim belonging to us. The following is a true story, and makes one's mouth water. A certain doctor, about to retire from the service, was tempted in an unguarded moment to offer £2,000 for a plantation, when times were at their very worst. Hardly had the auctioneer knocked it down to him when he became terrified at his own audacity; and greatly was he relieved when a general officer standing by offered to go halves with him. That estate now pays £10,000 a year clear profit, and the worthy pair are living at home in luxury.

I have been reading Sir Joseph Hooker's "Himalayan Journals," where he gives a most vivid description of Darjeeling and its neighbourhood, and in which, long before the days of the railroad, or the discovery of Mount Everest, he prophesied the great future which everyone now sees is certainly before it. This interesting book is now out of print, and a new edition urgently required.

All the carrying work in the place is done by coolies, and one is distressed to see very small children literally groaning under heavy loads of stones. You remark the great variety of races inhabiting the place: Lepchas, the aborigines of Sikkim, who believe in spirits good and bad, but celebrate no religious rites; Limboos, who are Buddhists; Moormis, grave, powerful men, originally from Thibet. The gold and silver ornaments worn by nearly all of them cannot fail to strike the stranger.

One morning five of us on ponies rode down to the Ging tea plantation, 2,500 feet below Darjeeling, to visit Mr. Durnford who manages it, and who is a friend of my friend,

Lady Crossley. The tea-plant is rather a pretty evergreen, resembling the myrtle or sweet bay more than any other shrub we have at home. It is not allowed to grow more than a foot and a half high. It was pruning season, and we could distinctly smell the tea aroma as we passed the gangs of Nepaulese workmen plying their knives. During December, January, and February they weed the ground and prune the plants. The leaves are picked in the nine remaining months: those on the very top, more like little stems than leaves, constituting the Pekoe, those immediately below them the Souchong-pekoe, and those nearer the centre of the bush the Souchong of commerce. They are all heated, rolled—first by machinery and secondly by hand—and then dried together, and afterwards passed through wires which separate the three qualities just mentioned. Then all imperfections are picked out by women, after which, the tea is packed in 80 lb. boxes made of toon wood, from Independent Sikkim, and carried up to Darjeeling by coolies, to be transmitted by railroad. The wages paid are good: 5r. 8a. for men, 4r. 8a. for women, and 3r.

for children per week. They are housed but not fed by the proprietors, who, however, generally give them plots of land on which to raise Indian corn, on which—and on rice—they subsist. The plants require no irrigation, as sufficient rain falls during the rainy season to nourish them. Their only enemy is the red spider, which has lately attacked them just as the phylloxera has done the vines in France. The new gardens are all adopting a hybrid between the Assam and the China plant, the former giving strength, the latter flavour. Mr. Durnford gave us at luncheon the only good curry I have tasted in India.

There were peals of thunder in the mountains as we rode up the hill, and at last once more in the evening we heard the sound of rain. "The clear shining after rain." I believed in that, consequently rose very early in the morning, and arrived at the point of view just as the first rays of the sun gilded the peak of Kinchinjunga. One after another, in proportion to their height, the other summits were lighted up till, by-and-bye, the whole mighty range of the eastern Himalayas for 200 miles stood revealed in unclouded splendour. The prospect is engraved in my mind for ever.

A great treat was awaiting us this morning. Mr. Prestage, the managing-director of the tram-line, had arranged that we should be "trollied" down the mountains instead of going in the train; so at Ghoom station, which is higher than Darjeeling, and from which to the plain there is a continuous descent, we found two little tram-cars fastened together, and Mr. Walker, one of the officials—a Scotchman, of course—who managed the brakes, and took us down in the most skilful manner, at the rate of fifteen miles an hour, stopping an hour for breakfast at the charming little Clarendon Hotel at Khersiong, from which we had our last look of the gigantic Kinchinjunga. The motion of the trollies was the most delightful I ever experienced in travelling, and without the locomotive you see the scenery far better. Its grandeur and variety struck us more than when going up.

At Siliguri station I saw a considerable

quantity of very superior jute, which had been brought on ox-carts for forty miles. We found here waiting us an excellent dinner, and three large sleeping-carriages for our night journey on the Northern Bengal Railway. The East Indian Company refused to give us any facilities whatever, but the managers of all the other railroads were exceedingly polite, and their liberality will certainly be an encouragement to travellers.

CHAPTER IX.

CALCUTTA, ITS BUILDINGS, TRADE, AND LIFE.

THE comparative cleanliness of the masses in India strikes me very forcibly. They are far superior in this respect to the inhabitants of Southern Europe, and their villages contrast most advantageously with those in Egypt and Syria. You find them performing their ablutions, with remarkable delicacy and propriety too, at every pond and brook; and, excepting at Benares, we have seen or smelt very little to offend.

The station-master at Siliguri told me that the fame of our large party—the only family one which ever travelled for pleasure in India—had for weeks preceded us, and that a native magistrate who had heard of, but had not believed in our numbers, had ridden eight miles to verify the report with his own eyes.

The great difficulty which all employers of European labour on railways, tea plantations, in mills, and elsewhere, have to contend against is the frequency with which even their most skilled and best servants get drunk. Perhaps they do it to drown care, or from weakness, or disappointment; but the fact remains, and it is a serious drawback to national progress. I find myself often thinking that, after all, India is a kind of banishment. No doubt salaries and wages are high; it may be, in a good many instances, too high. Certainly, people there can drive their carriages and enjoy many luxuries which could not be afforded at home; and we have met not a few cheerful souls who declare that life here is much preferable to life in England; but the general impression is the other way. Many little things make it stronger in my mind every week, and I feel less inclined than ever to think that Europeans of all classes employed in India, either in the public or private service, ought to be grudged their little luxuries.

Just after day-dawn we reached the Ganges, two-and-a-half miles broad, very shallow at the present season, and crossed it in the tidy, American-looking steamer, *Vampire.* What a multitude of birds we saw that forenoon—vultures, kites, herons, cranes, kingfishers, minas, pheasants, pigeons, bee-eaters, and countless others, the names of which I do not know, of varied and beautiful plumage, frequenting land and water. On many fields red capsicums were spread out to dry in the sun. In this part of Bengal you do not find that abject poverty which is so noticeable in other provinces of India. The houses of the poor are better, and they themselves seem better fed and clothed.

Between 12 and 1 we were in the Sealdah station, and this time went to the Great Eastern Hotel, a noisy, roughish place, but the best in Calcutta, where we remained for three days, preparatory to taking possession of 12, Elysium Row, which a fellow-passenger from England, Mr. Mackinnon, of the great shipping firm of Mackinnon, Mackenzie and Co., had with remarkable kindness placed at our disposal, for the celebration of a certain romantic marriage.

What a remarkable place this Calcutta is! The crowds, blocks, ox-carts, running coolies, dust and heat, in the busiest portion of it, overpower me. I observe in the weekly shipping list in the *Indian Daily News* for 22nd Jan., that there are no fewer than twenty-two large ocean-going steamers and seventy-eight sailing-ships from foreign ports lying in the river. Few people know that £30,000,000 sterling worth of goods are annually exported from Great Britain to India; that of the annual £75,000,000 worth of cotton goods exported £21,000,000 worth go to India, and that its foreign trade now amounts to very nearly £125,000,000.

We spent Saturday afternoon with Mr. Heriot, son of the late respected Sheriff of Forfarshire, who manages Howrah Jute Mills, on the other side of the river; and were glad to hear from him, and from Mr. Thom, of the Barnagore Works, where 5,000 people are employed, that there is no Sunday-work in any of these mills; and that, taking relays and other things into consideration, the people do not labour more than ten-and-a-half hours a day.

I was glad to hear the Rev. Mr. Gillan, of the Established Church of Scotland, preach in Union Chapel on Sunday morning.

On Monday morning I went with Mr. Payne, of the London Missionary Society, to see the idol-worship at Kalighat—the landing-place of Kali, from which Calcutta derives its name. It is now a suburb, situated on a branch of the Hooghly more sacred than the river itself, contains the holiest shrine in Bengal, and is as dirty as it is holy. There I found hundreds of poor bleating kids, with their legs cruelly tied together, which they first immerse in the sacred stream and then sacrifice before a hideous image of Kali, which was exposed for my inspection at the request of Mr. Payne, who is much beloved, notwithstanding his constant preaching of Christianity, by these poor people, and has so much influence with them that he induced a priest for one rupee to give me his upper garment, on which are written all the names of the Hindoo divinities. There also I beheld abominations, which cannot be recorded, confirmatory of the worst accounts given of iniquitous idolatry.

My next visit was to a very different place, not far off from the first, where 700 young men are receiving a general and Christian education of a very high order from the missionaries of the London Society. I examined one class, who in a few months were to matriculate for the University, and found them read and answer well. It is impossible that the teaching in these institutions should not produce a signal and widespread effect by-and-bye.

Since the foregoing sentence was written, I have had an opportunity of visiting the educational institutions connected with the Established Church and the Free Church of Scotland, and also an exceedingly well-conducted Christian girls' school in a very poor locality, over which Mrs. Macdonald presides. Mr. Hastie, the Principal of the General Assembly's scholastic establishment, was kind enough to conduct me through it; and I was glad to see the various classes of perhaps the most flourishing seminary of the kind in all India. There are 700 boys at the school and 500 students in the college, which, with 200 scholars outside and 600 girls in a separate building, make no fewer than 2,000 young people enjoying the advantage of an excellent education in Calcutta in connection with this church alone. Twenty-one youths out of the above number took the degree of B.A. at the last examination. The Free Church Mission had gone back a little; but no one doubts that under its new head, Mr. Robertson, it will soon add to its present number of 760. The Rev. Mr. Gillan, Presbyterian chaplain, and the Rev. Mr. Milne, Free Church clergyman, were good enough to accompany me, and I was interested to see the house where Dr. Duff so long lived and laboured.

I have now driven a great deal through Calcutta and its vicinity—which, by the way, is no joke, for the drivers, both of hackney carriages and of private vehicles, seem the worst in the world, and several accidents have taken place during our residence, two of them to friends of my own—and am much impressed with the magnitude of the place: the distances remind one of London. On the east of the Maidan are those spacious and often splendid bungalows from which it derives its name of the City of Palaces; but even close to them are little villages of native huts—one might almost call them wigwams; and although there are a considerable number of fine buildings, colleges, hospitals, Mahometan seminaries, and lofty residences of rich Baboos scattered throughout the native portion of the city, the streets present a mean appearance, and must impress a stranger fresh from Europe very unfavourably.

One evening we attended in Government House an investiture, first of the Star of India, and afterwards of the Indian Empire; at the close of which Lady Ripon had a reception. More than a thousand people were present, and the majority of the native dignitaries were gorgeously attired, some of them displaying an almost fabulous amount of jewellery. All classes in Hindostan are exceedingly extravagant, especially in the matter of ornament. Poor people will ruin themselves for life on the occasion of a marriage by borrowing, for the purpose of display. Many folks have their whole fortune invested in precious stones. The custom of Europeans is reckoned of little account in large towns, in comparison with that of rich natives, by jewellers and vendors of articles of luxury. One rajah spent lately, in Calcutta, in two months, £360,000.

It has been represented to me by men on whose judgment I rely, that British officers in India are required to do far too much clerk and office work; much time being occupied, in drawing up comparatively useless returns, which might be more profitably employed in purely military duties. Several of them likewise complain to me of the extravagance of the Government in building so many new barracks of expensive kiln-dried bricks, with roofs of teak, and other useless decorations; whilst in their opinion the old buildings, of the same material as the bungalows, confessedly immensely cheaper, are in many respects also better. They knew that many of the latter had been condemned by the Sanitary Department; but there are some facts and circumstances connected with this question which may necessitate a further inquiry.

An amusing anecdote in relation to this controversy was told to me. A distinguished Englishman travelling in the north-west thought he ought not to be contented with the testimony of officers, so he got up very early one morning and addressed a private soldier. "That is a very fine new barrack you inhabit." "Don't like it at all," was the reply. "But why?" he rejoined; "it has two stories, is exceedingly well-built and arranged, and gets all the air that is going in this hot climate." "Can't bear it notwithstanding," said the private. "That is curious," remarked the inquisitive stranger; "please tell me your reason." The man flatly refused for a long time; but at last, yielding to entreaty, roared out, "If you must know, I hate it because, when I gets drunk I can't get up the d—— stairs."

There is a somewhat delicate point which I do not like altogether to pass over, because excellent officers think it of some importance. Once a year the troops are called out to cheer for the Empress of India; and the native soldiers complain that whilst their European comrades are paid for doing so they are not. Surely this is an invidious distinction. Might not the payment be done away with? Or, better still, the whole ceremony dispensed with altogether?

On Friday the Rev. Mr. Johnson, of the London Missionary Society, asked a large number of native Christians to meet me at an evening party, when several speeches were made, and I addressed the audience, consisting of about one hundred, belonging to all sections of Protestants, and constituting really a Holy Catholic Church.

We must keep in mind that at the great educational institutions which I have been visiting there are few or no idlers. Only those who are anxious to learn attend; and their principal ambition is to get a good English education. This makes the task of the teachers comparatively easy.

CHAPTER X.

INDIA—MADRAS—COONOOR.

THE weather is now getting decidedly warm—warmer than usual, people tell me. On Saturday I did little but arrange for our departure, and go down in a steam-launch to the Botanical Gardens, where we drank the water from unripe cocoa-nuts under the shade of the celebrated banyan-tree. A last drive on the Maidan, and our party separated for a fortnight. I was one of those who slept on board the P. and O. steamer *Brindisi* at Garden Reach, which at daybreak dropped down the river, bound for Madras. *Slept*, indeed—the mosquitoes took good care to prevent that! They attacked us with a ferocity unheard of.

Although the banks of the Hooghly below Calcutta are flat, it is, nevertheless, a pretty sail. Vessels of all sizes and shapes, factories and plantations, give one constantly something to look at. At a point called, in vulgar parlance, the James and Mary, two large rivers flow into it, and the place reminded me much of various reaches on the Mississippi. Our pilot is a big man; gets about £2,000 per annum; and we were all greatly disappointed when, at mid-day, a little below Diamond Harbour, at Kalkee, he anchored for the night! And such a night! I tried the music-room, the saloon, the deck—all in vain. Myriads of mosquitoes followed, flew at, fastened on me in that damp, washing-house-like atmosphere, made my face and hands hideous, and rendered sleep a mockery.

At 2.30 a.m. Captain Lee (I wish all commanders of mail-steamers were as courteous and jolly, as well as omnipresent and attentive to their duties) and I met on deck in the fog; and it was a kind of cold comfort to find him as miserable as I was. At 8 a.m. the mist was still dense; and although only fifty-three miles from Calcutta, we had a close shave in getting off at all. Another half-hour's darkness would have detained us on that horrible bar for twenty-four hours more; but just as we sat down to breakfast the sun faintly appeared, the anchor was taken up, we pushed into a bank of fog, and emerged on the other side in a clear atmosphere, and proceeded at full speed down the great river, passing the outer light-ship at 3.30.

There is good pig-sticking on the right and tiger-shooting on the left bank of this Ganges mouth.

The *Brindisi* is a fine ship, only thirteen months old, not very fast—what P. and O. vessel is? their Indian contract is a premium to slowness—but comfortable; 3,500 tons burden; fitted with electric bells; steam steering gear, &c.; and, as "like master like man," all are civil and obliging on board. How delicious is this Indian Ocean! The air is heavenly! At noon on the last day of January we had run 270 miles in twenty-four hours, and were 422 miles from Madras.

I have been reading on the hurricane-deck all the forenoon Mr. Bose's book, "The Hindoos as they are," and am much interested in his testimony to the great change going on. Here are a few sentences, corroborative, I humbly think, of the impressions recorded from time to time in these notes :—

"The Hindoo schoolboy may be said from the day he entered a public school to enter on the first stage of his intellectual disintegration. The books that are put into his hands gradually open his eyes and expand his intellect; he learns to discern what is right and what is wrong; he reasons within himself and finds that what he had learnt at home was not true, and is led by degrees to renounce his old ideas."

"The progress of education has opened a new era in the social institutions of the country, and an enlightened proletariat is nowadays more esteemed than an empty-titled Dullaputty."

"Morally, socially and intellectually the enlightened Bengalees are assuredly the Athenians of Hindostan. Their growing intelligence and refined taste—the outcome of English education—have imbued them with a healthier ideal of moral excellence than any other section of the Indian population."

"As English schools and colleges are multiplying in every nook and corner of the empire, more liberal ideas and principles are being imbibed by the Hindoo youths, which bid fair in process of time to exercise a regenerating influence on the habits of the people. Idolatry, and its necessary concomitant, priestcraft, is fast losing its hold on their minds."

"The gigantic strides that English education has made in India within a short time have been the wonder of the age, the foundation-rock of her ultimate emancipation, socially, morally and intellectually."

"Some fifty or sixty years back, when English education could scarcely be said to have commenced the work of reformation, or rather disintegration . . . ."

"It is worthy of remark that though the distinction of caste still exerts its influence on all the important concerns of our social and domestic life, it is nevertheless fast losing its prestige in the estimation of the enlightened Hindoos."

"When Hindoo society is being profoundly convulsed by heterodox opinions . . . ."

The other side of the picture is, that the native intellect, quick in early years, stops developing very soon; and few attempt anything more after acquiring sufficient English and general information to ensure them employment. The medical schools, they tell me, are becoming a rapidly-increasing educational power.

The 1st of February has come, and with it great heat. At noon we were in latitude 14° 48′, longitude 82° 19′; and, having run 272 miles, were only 150 miles from Madras, and consequently had to slacken speed, as we could not go in before daylight. There is a decided swell, but no air, far less wind. We have a number of coolies in the forecastle, returning from Demerara. Some of them have been twenty years there.

I rose at 5.30 on Thursday morning, and saw the revolving light at Madras harbour. By-and-bye the mist rolled away, the sun rose, and a long line of white houses, a shattered breakwater, and many ships at anchor showed us that our voyage was terminated. Then what a row the naked crews of the shore-boats made: greater, I think, than I had ever witnessed, even in the Levant. Catamarans, constructed merely of three logs tied together, were paddled round the ship when the anchor went down, and in a few moments the deck was crowded by porters and boatmen scrambling for custom. An A.D.C. from Government House delivered us from these Philistines; and after a drive of eight miles in the delicious morning air, we were welcomed at Guindy Park House by my distinguished friend Mr. Grant Duff, whose cultivated intellect, large official experience, love of work, and knowledge of India cannot fail to be of essential service to the inhabitants of the Presidency.

Madras is not a town, but a population of 400,000, scattered over twenty-seven miles. Its palatial buildings, wide avenues, and open spaces surprise me. It has quite the air of a capital; and trees as well as costumes remind us that we are a good deal nearer the equator.

Guindy Park is five miles in circumference; and we look over its spreading trees to rounded and peaked hills in the distance—a refreshing prospect after the dull monotony of North India's plains. There are cobras within the compound; and only last week they killed, close to the house, a Russell viper—the most poisonous of all snakes. The beauty and variety of the gardens here are celebrated. The bread-fruit, cocoa-nut, palms, jack-fruit, and many other striking forest trees, plants, and flowers interest me much. The park is full of deer, and also of jackals.

We drove about until we could no longer see on the evening of our arrival; and there was a large dinner-party, attended, amongst others, by the Maharajah of Travancore; and a number of Hindoo and Mahommedan gentlemen came afterwards, when the lawn and terrace were illuminated—a very pretty sight.

Next morning early Mr. Grant Duff and I

drove to St. Thomas' Mount, the artillery cantonment; and after breakfast I went into Madras, called on Messrs. Arbuthnot and Co., and from the top of their offices had a very commanding view of the native quarter, called Blacktown, the fort, port, and shipping. Before sundown we had a long drive through paddy-fields and dense masses of palms, paid a visit to the Botanical Gardens—where there is much that is curious and interesting—to Government House, near the sea, and to the stables at Guindy. Nearly all the carriage-horses in India—Walers, as they are called—come from Australia. It is now very hot; and although occasionally the sea-breeze comes up, I begin to wish for a cooler atmosphere.

On Saturday evening we drove to the artillery parade-ground, at the foot of St. Thomas's Mount, where a large company of Europeans and natives had assembled to witness athletic sports, and a very lively and picturesque sight it was. The horse artillery driving through gates and over hurdles reflected the greatest credit on the batteries. Then we had a dinner-party of forty-four, a ball, and another illumination in the evening: our last in Madras. I would rather live in Guindy Park than in any other house which I have seen in India.

On Sunday I was really afraid to go to church, so powerful were the sun's rays. We left at 6 p.m. in the mail-train for the hills. The station at Madras is a very imposing one of red brick, with a lofty tower, perhaps the most conspicuous object in the place. Nothing could exceed the kindness we experienced at the hands of the officials in reserving carriages for us, keeping them waiting where we stopped, and showing an example to their brethren of the East Indian. We all slept well, as there was less motion than on any line by which we have travelled in the country. They have adopted an excellent plan of selling dinner and breakfast tickets when you pay your fare; they thus know and can wire how many are to be provided for, and have likewise a protection against dishonest "butlers," as they call them at the refreshment rooms.

We dined at Arconum, and when I awoke

we were passing through a very rich country with luxuriant crops, although the cultivation seemed of an exceedingly primitive description. Many women were working in the fields. By-and-bye ranges of peaked hills came in sight, and we stopped for breakfast at Poothanoor, where a branch to the hills joins the Beypoor main line. The viands were poor, and the waiting was simply scandalous. Most of us had to help ourselves.

Just before Coimbatoor station there is a view of remarkable beauty—a lake or "tank" in the foreground, palms beyond, and behind rugged, jagged peaks of infinite variety. Strange and picturesque indeed was the whole scene—the gay colours of the peasants' scanty garments, the thick aloe hedges—everything so different from Northern India. There are quantities of the prickly pear here, many plantations of the graceful castor-oil plant, rice, grain, beans, tobacco, and cotton, with rows of fine forest trees. Then the line descends through a waste-land region into a kind of basin, and terminates at Matipolliam, where we were transferred into three "tongas"—a kind of rough, low, two-wheeled dog-cart, drawn by two ponies, which are attached, not by traces, but by a short high pole with a bar across their backs. In these we reached Coonoor, upwards of twenty miles in 3¼ hours; the ponies were changed four times and trotted all the way, although the rise is more than 6,000 feet. The road was crowded with carts, oxen, and coolies, and many a sharp curve and turn made us quake, as in most places there is no parapet. The vegetation is exceedingly varied in colour, luxuriant and beautiful, and every now and then we had extensive views over the great plain below, studded with isolated hills like islands.

Four or five miles from our destination we saw coffee plantations for the first time, and before 2 o'clock were in Gray's Hotel: a pretty bungalow—like a cottage in Devonshire—embowered in roses and heliotrope, on a hill 600 feet above Coonoor (itself 6,100 above the sea), and commanding a wide prospect of mountains wild as those of Scotland. The first thing that strikes me in reaching this very beautiful and homelike place is the extent to which the eucalyptus appears on every slope. They have been planted principally for fuel, but also for shade. Mr. Jamieson, who takes charge of the gardens and plantations at Ootakamund, and who has been most attentive to us, tells me that trees which he put in only four years ago are already sixty feet high. He says that Australian and Tasmanian trees flourish in these hills, but not the deciduous trees or pines of Britain.

We spent Tuesday morning very pleasantly on Mr. Allan's coffee plantation of Glenmore, where he employs 200 men, all Canarese, from Mysore. They go home for about two months in the slack season, and get 6r. 8a. per week—an excellent wage. The coffee-plant is kept at a height of 3½ feet, has leaves a little like a Portugal laurel, and a very thick stem, resembling that of a tree several years old. The berries are red when ripe, and called cherries. The bean is separated from the husk by simple machinery, driven by a water-wheel. The leaf disease, which has caused such havoc in the Ceylon plantations, has only threatened to

PLAIN IN SOUTHERN INDIA.

appear here; as yet no serious damage has been done.

In the afternoon we drove to see the great view over the South Indian plain from the summit of the mighty slopes of the Neilgherries. There are three principal points—Lamb's Rock, Lady Canning's Seat, and Dolphin's Nose. The narrow and rough road, in driving along which we experienced much difficulty when we met ox-carts, passes sometimes through thick tropical vegetation, where creepers of many kinds abound, the crimson flower of the rhododendron tree—not shrub—being at this season conspicuous. Sometimes the road winds round unfenced promontories with yawning gulfs below, and again looks down on tea-gardens planted wherever the ground is not actually precipitous. The views of the hills and plain far below are very grand.

A company of Todas, the aboriginal and fast dying out pastoral inhabitants of the range, were sent to see us at sundown. They are a very peculiar people, practise infanticide and polyandry, and live in low huts into which they have to crawl. They refuse to do any work but tend cattle.

CHAPTER XI.

CONJEVERAM—DEPARTURE FROM MADRAS.

ON Wednesday morning we left for Ootakamund, passing the race-course and the spacious Wellington Barracks; and after leaving the plantations of Coonoor emerging into a bleak, red, treeless country very much resembling Algeria. The road is well made. We changed horses often, trotted all the way up, and came down at a rattling pace, drawn sometimes by mere ponies. I never was charged so high a bill in any part of the world as that of the Madras Carrying Company.

At Charing Cross, Colonel Iago, head of the Woods Department, met us and took us first to Government House, not a successful building, where I was anxious to see the room in which my lamented friend Mr. Adam died, and I afterwards reverently visited his grave in the new churchyard: a pretty spot, overlooking the lake.

The Botanical Gardens are full of interesting trees, shrubs and flowers. One of the loveliest of the last is of that detestable medicine called jalap. The Chinese rice-paper tree is remarkable. I took away with me a portion of the stem from which paper is made. On a hill above Coonoor there is a wood looking at a distance exactly like a plantation of Scotch firs seventy years old: it is eucalyptus aged eleven. The Chinchona plantations of Government on the Neilgherries, one of which adjoins the garden at Ootakamund, are very important and prosperous; they cover 800 acres, cost last year in labour £96,000, and their gross produce was £300,000. The value of the bark after the wound has been medicated by wet moss, is twice as great as before the knife has been first applied. We lunched at the Cedars, the beautiful residence of Mr. Barlow, Collector of the district, the drawing-room window of which commands a fine view of the Kundah range; this is more picturesque than the huge rounded Doddabett, 8,622 feet above the sea, which rises behind Government House. There are many tigers in these mountains, and Mr. Barlow had in his hall a magnificent head of a Sambur stag, which he shot six weeks ago, close by.

"Ooty," as it is familiarly called, is 7,300 feet above the sea. I distinctly perceived the rarefaction of the air. We returned by a very pretty drive past the Lawrence Asylum for Boys, which joins the main road at the top of the hill, where you look down both on Ootakamund and Coonoor.

Mr. Jamieson kindly sent down to the Government gardens at the foot of the hills for mangosteen for our dessert. I thought the fruit delicious, like a very delicate French confection.

Next morning we descended the ghâut at a tremendous pace; and at a sudden turn the vehicle which conveyed me collided with a tonga on its way to Coonoor. The crash was alarming, but no damage resulted. Matipolliam is a veritable Gehenna for heat; but at the station house there were washing-rooms, kept scrupulously clean; and we enjoyed an excellent luncheon at the adjacent dâk bungalow. We did not penetrate farther south in India than

Poothanoor junction—about 700 miles from the equator.

We dined at Salem, and had a miserable hour at Arconum, between 4 and 5 o'clock in the morning, stowing away our effects in the left luggage-room—as the station-master refused to allow them to remain in our reserved carriage—and in endeavouring to get washed.

At 5.15 a.m. we left, in the Southern India narrow-gauge railway, for Conjeveram, seventeen miles off, and, when we arrived there, fancied that some celebration was going on, as the station was crowded with servants in red liveries, policemen, native magistrates, &c., and two or three hundred spectators lined its approaches. My surprise was great when, on stepping out, wreaths of yellow and pink chrysanthemums were thrown round our necks, strange bird-like devices, chiefly of the same material, and limes were placed in our hands, and all bowed low to do us honour. Few Europeans visit Conjeveram; hence the gaping and admiring crowd! Tea was ready for us at the station; and then we set out to visit the temples, in covered carts drawn by oxen, which trotted along merrily.

Conjeveram is a clean, well-kept place, with wide streets and a thriving population. One who has travelled in eastern Europe and western Asia remarks how few deformed people there are in India in comparison. The sight of a cripple and a woman afflicted with elephantiasis during our drive reminded me of this. At one turn of the road we came on a huge car, exactly like that of Juggernaut, and like it, also, happily laid up in ordinary. We likewise visited an immense tank, one of the most sacred in India, containing a mixture of holy waters.

We first drove to Vishnu's temple, in Little Kanchi, and were received by a crowd of priests and spectators, fireworks and music, and entertained with a nautch-girl dance, after which we inspected the wealth of jewels, and had all the hideous idols brought out to view. The hall of pillars, in the centre of the enclosure, is very remarkable for carved horses and hippogriffs; and the whole scene was one of the most strange and striking which we witnessed in India. The other famous temple—that dedicated to Seva the Destroyer—has a gopura, or great tower, 181 feet high—the highest in Southern India—and there we were received in a similar manner; but its buildings did not strike us as so curious as those of the first; and thirty years ago it was robbed of its principal jewels. Its frightful idols are carried in procession on high days. They give one a sad idea of heathenism—its brutalising and degrading nature. "Jehovah dwells not in temples made with hands." May the millions of Hindostan soon realise the blessings of a purer, holier and manlier religion!

Formerly these temples were managed by the British Government; and by gifts to them officials foolishly thought to propitiate the Hindoo people. The Mutiny and other events roughly opened our eyes to the inefficacy of such a cowardly policy; and now this idol-worship has no connection with the State. Complaint has recently been made that the new law in this respect has been infringed in the case of a well-known temple in the Punjaub;

but I have reason to believe that what took place there has been disapproved at head-quarters, and that no such breach of the order will be permitted in future. It may also be well for the central Government to keep an eye on those in authority who refuse to employ natives if they happen to profess Christianity.

Our visits to the temples over, we were driven to the Tahsildar's bungalow, to which servants, with all the materials requisite for a sumptuous breakfast and luncheon, had been sent all the way from Madras by the thoughtful care of Mr. Grant Duff and his genial staff, who had, I need scarcely add, likewise given orders to the officials to receive us at the station and pay us every attention. This is the only place we have been in in India without seeing a European or even a Eurasian. The gentleman who took charge of us was the Deputy Tahsildar of Chingleput district—Mr. Damodera Maodilly—and most kind and attentive he was.

Returning to Arconum, we dined, and joined the evening mail-train from Madras to Bombay.

When I awoke, we were at the old ruined fort of Gooty. In every field there was a man in a structure elevated on poles, watching the crops and protecting them against the depredations of wild beasts. We passed much waste-land—the country was quite flat, with low and generally isolated hills at a distance, and, nearer to the line, singular rocky mounds, rising to a considerable height at the town of Adoni—then we crossed the now nearly dry channel of the river Toongabudra, which joins the Beema some distance below, and the two together form the Kistna. The cactus makes an excellent railway-fence in Southern India.

At Raichoor the Madras Railway ends and the Great Indian Peninsular begins. We arrived there at 11.30; and, having had nothing since the previous evening but a cup of weak tea, were naturally hungry. What was our astonishment when told there was no breakfast ready at a place where we were to stop forty minutes, except a piece of cold beef covered with wire and flies! Some one used an unparliamentary expression, and, hey, presto! appeared one of the best breakfasts we had had set before us in India—choice tea, excellent curry, tender mutton chops and fresh eggs. Where it came from must remain a mystery for ever.

CHAPTER XII.

AT POONA.

WE are now in the Nizam's territory, and a branch line goes off at Wadi to his capital of Hyderabad. Rising to a higher level, the line passes over a poorly-cultivated and sparsely-peopled district, with extensive tracts of waste-land. It was very hot all day: even the venetians failed to keep out the sun's rays; and we felt the lightest of clothing too heavy, and motion impossible. Dining at Sholapore, we reached Poona at 4.40 a.m., and found carriages and servants waiting to take us to join the other members of our party in the Napier Hotel.

We heard an admirable sermon from the Rev. Mr. Small, of the Free Church of Scotland, on Sunday evening; and on Monday forenoon paid two visits of great interest to me.

There are six Government schools for females in Poona, over which Mrs. Mitchell and her very energetic assistant, Miss Rosa Morris, preside.

J 2

They commenced only ten years ago; but already have sent forth a great number of teachers; and now none are admitted into the higher classes, or those for schoolmistresses only, who have not passed the third standard in the vernacular. On entering that college they get a salary varying from two to eight rupees per month, dependent on length of attendance and progress.

We spent a long time in the principal of these schools; and were greatly gratified by all we saw and heard. Little girls are brought in, on whom the young teachers first try their hand; then the latter are sent out to give instruction in other institutions, still under the eye of their European superiors; and lastly they are available for situations anywhere. I was delighted with Miss Morris's "Marathi Songs for Children," one of them set to music to the old familiar tune of "Duncan Gray." It was remarkable to see the transformation worked by this able and enthusiastic young lady on the silent, motionless Hindoo youngsters: they were all life and joy when following her lead.

Many of the women—some of them mere children—are widows; and the popular feeling is much opposed to their being taught and teaching.

Our second visit was to the old palace of the Peishwas' commander-in-chief—now turned to a much better purpose—a school in which 300 young men and boys are taught under the superintendence of Mr. Beaumont, of the Free Church of Scotland. Two hundred learn English, and the good attendance and anxiety to learn were very evident. From the roof of the building I had an excellent view of Poona, with its neat and clean native town of 80,000 inhabitants, the cantonment, public buildings, and officers' bungalows, situated in a basin surrounded by hills.

This morning the Royal Commission on Education, the names of its members, and the instructions to them of the Governor-General in Council, appear in the newspapers, and to my mind the expressed views and orders of the Government appear eminently satisfactory. The extension of primary education to the masses is set forth as the main desideratum of the present day. Hitherto we have been doing rather too much to instruct, at the expense of the State, classes well able to pay for their own education, and not overloyal, or likely in certain contingencies and in certain respects not to make a very good use of it.* I anticipate much good from this enquiry and new departure. Government has likewise, I see with pleasure, taken up seriously the recommendations of the Famine Commission, of which my friend Mr. James Caird, C. B., was a leading member, which some feared might be allowed to fall into neglect. A new department is to be formed, which will put the rulers of India in possession of all the necessary facts regarding the food supplies, and likewise give an impetus to agricultural improvement, and so render famines less likely and disastrous. I hope that those charged with this important duty will give a

* "Too much money is spent by the Government in giving to the richer classes a superior education for which they ought to pay themselves, while too little is spent on elementary instruction for the masses of the poor." "The Finances and Public Works of India," by Sir J. Strachey and Major-General R. Strachey. London, Kegan Paul, French & Co.

favourable consideration to Mr. W. Wedderburn's scheme for the formation of Agricultural Banks, which seems already to have commended itself to the Government of Bombay. He has published a most interesting and readable pamphlet on the subject, in which he narrates what has been done in Germany; points out that "the fundamental error of what has hitherto been done in India consists in the attempt to accomplish through State agency what can only be successfully carried out by private enterprise;" and in a most business-like manner propounds, explains, and defends his own plan; which certainly commends itself to my judgment as one which, if adopted and extensively acted upon, cannot fail to be an enormous boon to India.

We are all constantly being reminded in various ways of the poverty of the people, and the primary necessity of improving their lot. I am no defender of the Government interest in opium; and no one I imagine would, if such a mode of raising revenue were proposed as a new measure, care to defend it; but it is very questionable if China would be morally benefited by a change of system which might greatly extend the cultivation of the poppy; and I say without hesitation that the poor ryots of India have a prior claim on us for a reduction, and let it be hoped eventually the abolition, of the salt-tax, which presses on the very poorest of the population, and has been, I believe fairly, estimated as equal to a fortnight's labour per annum of every head of a family who earns his bread by the sweat of his brow.

We drove on Monday evening to the enormous pile of buildings erected at most unjustifiable cost as a Government residence at Gunesh Khind, then through the Kirkee cantonment of artillery and sappers and miners, across the bridge where the river has been dammed up so as to form a pretty lake, and home by the public gardens. The Southern Cross shines gloriously here in early morning at present. When we arrived from the south at 4.30 a.m., its stars were like lamps to our path.

There is an extensive view of Poona and its surroundings from the Temple of Parbuttee, or Goddess of Love, situated on a lofty rock close to the town; and the prettiest place within a short drive is Sungum, where the rivers Moota and Moola meet close to the Bombay railroad line.

Many questions are likely to be asked of those who have travelled in India regarding the probable stability of British power. It must be kept in mind that there is no such thing as patriotism or national feeling among the heterogeneous races which form the population of Hindostan, and that the millions of ryots and labourers neither love nor hate us, but simply view our reign with indifference, in fact think and care little about us. There are Mahommedan fanatics, who do cherish deep-seated dislike to us, both on religious and political grounds; and certain Brahmins may sympathise more or less with them; and the events of the Mutiny showed how badly-informed the official class was at the time as to the state of public feeling; and how foolish men in authority were in refusing to listen to the representations and warnings of the missionaries. But there are two considerations which render a fresh outbreak unlikely. In the first place, thousands of the upper classes among the natives are fast making money under our régime of law and order; and, secondly, such military arrangements have been made since 1857 as render a successful insurrection almost impossible. All the forts are in European hands, and all the artillery, with the exception of a few small batteries in the north-west frontier, is in the same position. Everyone, however, admits that there is a danger from the armies kept up by native princes, which are absolutely useless and very expensive, and may give trouble. Careful but vigorous steps should be taken to reduce their number, which stands at present on paper at 381,000 men, most of whom, however, are a mere rabble, although Scindia has adopted the German system, and could at any time call out a large, well-disciplined force. It would be difficult, if not impossible, to induce rajahs to dismiss men who had once "eaten their bread;" but might not the paramount power insist on enlistment being reduced and eventually stopped?

I fain hope and believe that a very marked

improvement has taken place in the treatment of the natives by Europeans. There are no doubt many stories afloat, some of them perhaps more or less true, and some much exaggerated, of the unjust decisions of judges, the violent behaviour of officers, and the supercilious conduct of men in authority; but I find testimony wonderfully unanimous in favour of the present rather than the past; and those on whose judgment most reliance can be placed all say, Deliver us from the old school—the "Qui hais" of the last generation—and send us out gentlemen from England fresh to their duties, who will not be so tyrannical and capricious as those who in so many instances have reflected no credit on the British name. No one can be long in India and visit its courts of law without observing how closely, almost ridiculously, the various customs, disputes, and lawsuits about land in that country resemble those in Ireland. The great difficulty with the natives seems to be their disregard of truth, and their habit of exaggeration; all their statements must be put in writing or they would be denied on the first convenient opportunity.

Perhaps the most important question of the hour is how to place the tenure of land on a more satisfactory footing. Nor can we afford to overlook the natural desire expressed by the educated classes for an extension of the representative principle. The great council of Calcutta *has been* almost in abeyance, and *is now* not much of a reality. It may be possible, by-and-bye, to strengthen it by delegates from successfully-managed municipalities, or in some other manner to meet an ever-increasing demand. As a fair example of the feelings and opinions of the natives, I cannot do better than insert here a copy of an address presented to me at a meeting of the Sarvajanik Sabha attended by 800 or 1,000 people in Poona, on the evening before I left.

"HON. SIR,—It gives us great satisfaction to have the privilege of welcoming you on behalf of the native public of this place. You have always been honourably distinguished by your adhesion to liberal principles, and you have been one of that small band of Englishmen who have always evinced an interest in Indian matters.

Since the days of the Mutiny and the assumption of direct sovereignty over India by Her Majesty the Queen-Empress the affairs of India have assumed their natural place in the thoughts of Englishmen, and, however much the leaders of both parties in Parliament profess to regard Indian questions as out of the pale of party politics, during the last four or five years especially Indian grievances and wrongs have furnished a considerable number of topics on which the Parliament and the public of England have felt themselves called upon to interest themselves as intimately as if they were purely English questions. Under these circumstances it becomes the duty of those who have India's welfare at heart to supply from time to time, as occasion arises, correct information of the views and wants of the people of this country, and to seek to influence the English public through its recognised leaders in the English Parliament and the English Press. In this connection it is felt by us all to be a most fortunate circumstance that hon. Members of Parliament avail themselves of the small leisure at their disposal to visit this distant country, and make themselves practically acquainted with its material and moral condition. Official sources of information are always at your disposal, and we, under existing conditions, can hope but little to supplement it with accurate statistics and other detailed information. At the same time you cannot but be fully aware that official authorities, however honest and painstaking, are seldom able to grasp all sides of the questions that come before them, and certain it is that they do not possess the same facilities to know where the official machine presses hard upon the people as intelligent representatives of the people themselves may be expected to do. The absence of any representative institutions, even of a consultative character, to control and modify the action of executive officers, enhances the difficulty caused by the differences of race, religion and manners between the rulers and the ruled. It is, however, a hopeful circumstance that notwithstanding these difficulties India has made a fair progress in good government during the twenty-five years that have passed since the Mutiny troubles. The force of Indian public opinion is, however, so small that it needs to be strengthened by the active sympathy and co-operation of India's friends in Parliament. It is with this view that we have troubled you with this call upon your valuable time, and we cannot but express our heartfelt thanks for your accepting our invitation with such cordial readiness. Allow us, in the short time that is at your disposal, to briefly note for your attention a few points on which we feel that in the interests of England and India the administrative machinery set up in this country fails to give satisfaction to the people, and requires to be carefully looked after, with a view to adapt it to the wants of the present day. We freely acknowledge all the benefits which British rule has secured to this country in maintaining undisturbed tranquility and guaranteeing its safety against foreign invasions, in encouraging education, in developing a system of useful public works, and the other benefits incident to a high state of civilisation. While in all these respects there has been great progress during the last twenty-five years, the form of the administration and its direct action upon the people have remained for the most part unchanged. It is true that Legislative Councils for the more advanced provinces were constituted in 1861; but their constitution is so one-sided, and their power so limited, that in the hands of strong rulers they have almost ceased to possess any influence for good, and are too often made the instruments of registering official wishes without being able to represent outside opinion effectively. The attention of Indian reformers has of late been directed to this question, and various schemes have been suggested with a view to improve the constitution of these councils. The absence of any local organisations which could be trusted with the power of electing representatives has been always felt to be a very serious want ; but the extension of the decentralisation policy by the present Government of India will, we trust, supply this want by the creation of self-governing municipalities and district local boards. Mr. William Digby has recently published a pamphlet, in which he insists, with good reason, upon the urgent necessity of this reform, as lying at the root of all other reforms in Indian administration. We are fully aware that constitutional habits and traditions take a long time to grow and cannot be created to order. At the same time we assure you that the establishment of some correlation between the views of the Indian public and the British rulers is a necessity which Parliament will have to direct its attention to if the present process is not to be retarded. The people of India will be satisfied at present with the establishment of a consultative assembly, consisting of officials and non-officials, the latter representing the large towns and districts, with a right to be consulted in matters of new legislation and taxation, and of interpellating executive officers with a view to elicit information upon administrative details.

"2. Next in importance to the reform noted above is the liberalising of local administrations in the large towns and more advanced districts. The Government of India has already in the series of resolutions expressed itself strongly in favour of extending local self-government. The official authorities, however, viewing the matter from their own stand-point, will, it is feared, not co-operate with the same singleness of purpose which earnest conviction alone secures. English opinion has alone the power to remove these obstacles, and we trust that those who have the ear of the English public in and out of Parliament will strengthen the hands of the Government of India to secure the success of their contemplated reforms.

"3. It is not without reason that we have drawn your attention to the necessity which exists of English public opinion coming to our assistance. In the settlement of the much-disputed land question the authorities in India, as well as the Secretary of State, as far back as 1862, definitively pronounced themselves in favour of extending the permanent settlement in all the more settled districts of the country. Owing to local opposition, however, that despatch, though not formally overruled, has remained a dead letter to this day. The example of bad native rulers, who enhanced the assessments arbitrarily at times, has been turned into an argument to support the policy of periodical re-settlements, and a great deal too much is made of the concession of this modified system of conferring interest in land upon the peasantry. The fact, however, is that the best native rulers respected and recognised indefeasible property in land, subject to a fixed charge, and, what in England is called freehold, was the common tenure of this country, with the name of *mirasi*, as typical of the highest property that a man can possess. Whatever may be the theory, the Government assessment absorbs not a portion of the rent proper, but the whole of the rent and a portion of the profits of cultivation. As a consequence of this state of things the country is reduced to a dead level of poverty. Two Commissions appointed by Government (the Deccan

Riots Commission of 1875, and the Famine Commission of 1878-79) have set forth the evils of the present system, and the independent members in those two Commissions have to a great extent endorsed the views we have long entertained on the subject. A modified permanent settlement, which will secure its due share to Government in the land revenue, is as important to the future growth of this country as the settlement of the Irish land question is in Ireland.

"4. Another question in which the people of India have always evinced the greatest interest, and have repeatedly memorialised Parliament for the redress of their grievances, is the question of the admission of the natives on equal terms with Englishmen in the ranks of the covenanted services. The Covenanted Civil Service was thrown open to public competition in 1853, but it was not till 1864 that the first native candidate passed the tests. Soon after, the limit of age was reduced from 23 to 21, but it did not materially interfere with the chances of native candidates finding admission into the service. And in ten years, from 1867 to 1877, about twelve more candidates passed the test. In 1878 the limit of age was still further lowered to 19, from which time no Indian candidate has found it possible to appear at the examination. This limit of 19 was, we understand, disapproved by a large majority of the authorities consulted, and is found very inconvenient even in the case of English candidates. Indian opinion, while insisting upon the test of examinations and the advantage of residence in England, only asked that the examinations should be held in India and in England subject to the same tests. This prayer was refused, and in its place the late Viceroy has sought to satisfy native claims by the creation of a subordinate native service, distinctly marked as separate from the governing body by differences in pay, prospects and promotion, and not chosen by competition, but by nomination from considerations of family connections. This we regard to be a distinctly retrograde step, and native public opinion will not be satisfied till a return is made to the old liberal rules. Next to the Covenanted Civil Service, the largest opening to native ambition is furnished by the rules of the medical service. We trust there is no foundation for the report that English authorities contemplate the abolition of these examinations, and substituting in their stead a system of direct nomination from the medical schools in England. The admission of natives into the ranks of the military service has long been felt to be a desideratum, especially in the case of the scions of the noble families for whom this career would furnish a healthy occupation. The late Army Commission has recommended the partial adoption of this reform in the case of Bengal and Punjab, and we trust that India's friends in Parliament will press this subject upon the attention of the authorities till this invidious distinction between class and class is removed.

"5. The threatened abolition of the cotton duties, and the necessity which will soon be forced upon the Indian authorities of surrendering some portion of their opium revenue in deference to the anti-opium agitation, renders the position of Indian finance so unstable, that notwithstanding the anticipated surplus of this year it will be impossible to make both the ends meet without effecting retrenchments in all departments. The highest military authorities who were represented in the Army Commission suggested a reduction of one and a half million sterling in the army expenditure. An equal sum might be saved by the larger substitution of native for European agency in the police, public works, medical, educational, post office and account branches, in which there are at present no vested interests to conserve. In this connection the reduction of the home charges by a more equitable distribution of the Indian army expenditure in England, and the purchase of the stores in the local markets, will also commend themselves to you as requiring immediate attention. If in addition to these reductions England guarantees the interest of Indian public debt, as it is bound to do in its own interest, the total reductions will amount to about five millions sterling, which will be a great relief, and might enable India to bear with equanimity the partial loss of the opium revenue, and the total loss of the cotton duties. We need hardly urge upon your attention that there is little or no room for additional taxation in this country, where the people are so poor that the chief necessary of life has to be taxed a thousand-fold to the great inconvenience of all classes, and that an income-tax on the English scale is expected to yield only one million sterling. The existing license tax has been condemned for its invidious incidence, and also for the poverty of its return, while the other heads of revenue are already fixed at their highest pitch. The reduction of expenditure is thus not a question of choice, but of necessity for the success of Indian finance.

"6. In the same connection we are glad to note that the question of the disestablishment of the Anglo-Indian Church has already engaged your attention. The services of army chaplains must be secured under any circumstances, but the same necessity cannot be pleaded for the diversion of public funds for the support of the four bishoprics and a large number of chaplains who minister to the spiritual wants of the wealthy amongst the European civil population. Having due regard to the promises contained in the great Royal Proclamation of 1858, the natives of this country must demand that this abuse of State funds shall be put a stop to forthwith, and we trust that when the time comes, you will support our prayer for the abolition of this anomaly before Parliament.

"7. In submitting the foregoing observations on this occasion we are fully conscious that the questions indicated therein have complex bearings, and the point of view from which we look at them must be modified by other considerations which commend themselves to the Indian authorities. It seems, therefore, to us to be very necessary that all the bearings of the questions should be sifted by an independent commission of inquiry. In the last session of Parliament Mr. Fowler and Sir David Wedderburn made a motion to this effect, and we have good reasons to think that but for the Irish distractions the Prime Minister and the Secretary of State for India would have accepted a limited enquiry. We trust that when the arrears of home business are cleared, you and the other friends of India will re-open this question. Periodical enquiries into the working of the Indian Government have produced good results in the past, and the time appears to us to have come when such an enquiry might be expected to lead to similar results in the future.

"8. We hope to be excused for the length over which these observations have extended. The Liberal party at present in power, and of which you are so distinguished a member, pledged their word at the late elections to accomplish certain reforms in accordance with the expressed wishes of the people of this country. They have given us peace on the frontiers; they have set a noble precedent in defraying a portion, though a small one, of the cost of the Afghan war from the English revenues; they have sent his Excellency the Marquis of Ripon to rule over us, and deputed Major Baring to manage our finances. These Indian authorities have earned a title to the confidence of the country by stimulating private enterprise, encouraging the consumption of articles of indigenous manufactures, setting free the Indian vernacular press, and laying down a scheme for the extension of local self-government These generous concessions have laid the people under great obligations to the leaders of the Liberal party, and we request that you will convey this expression of our gratitude to the Right Hon. Mr. Gladstone, the Right Hon. the Marquis of Hartington, and the Right Hon. Mr. Bright, and Mr. Fawcett, for their noble endeavours to promote the best interests of this country."

CHAPTER XIII.

RETURN TO BOMBAY.

I HAD occasion, on the 15th, to send a telegram to Scotland, and received an answer, *viâ* Bombay, in seven hours! The Post Office and Telegraphic services in India are most admirably conducted. In 1880-81 no fewer than 159,000,000 of letters, newspapers and parcels passed through the Post Office, and nearly 15,000,000 of post-cards were used. In the course of the same year nearly £8,000,000 worth of insured property was sent through the Post Office, of which only £1,040 was lost.

The most conspicuous building in Poona is the synagogue, its lofty red tower being seen from every point of view. The principal street in the native town is wider and has much handsomer and cleaner houses than is the case in most Indian towns: it resembles one in an American western city. Sugar-cane is extensively grown in the vicinity, there being an ample supply of water to irrigate the fields; and it pays better than other crops.

At 12.30 on 16th February we left by train for Bombay. At this time of year the country on the route is more dreary and burnt-up than any we had seen in India. The bare conical hills have a Scotch-like appearance.

In a little over two hours we arrived at the beginning of the descent of the famous Bhore Ghâut, one of the most remarkable engineering feats in the world, and were detained a long time by a landslip, which had blocked the line shortly before, near Kundala. In a very few miles the railway descends more than 1,800 feet. At one point there is a reversing station, the engine changing its position. There are many tunnels; and the views of the plain far down below—of overhanging peaks, deep gorges and precipices—are very fine. The fact of there being more deciduous trees than usual on these slopes detracts from the beauty of the scenery in the winter. At Callianee Junction, where the Calcutta line branches off, there are some very fantastically-shaped hills; and here are the prettiest station garden and flowers which we had seen in India.

Bombay strikes one, on returning to it, as, after all, in point of public buildings and streets, much the handsomest town in the country. About Elphinstone Circle and the Esplanade it will in these respects bear comparison with some European capitals; and the drive round Cumballa and Malabar hills, among the delightful bungalows, which overlook the Indian Ocean on the north, and get the benefit of its refreshing breezes, is one of the most beautiful of its kind anywhere to be seen.

On Sunday I went out to Parek, to lunch with Sir James Fergusson, the able Governor of the Presidency, who, on account of severe domestic affliction, had not been able to ask us to stay with him, as proposed; and in the evening we attended divine service at the Free Church of Scotland.

At Agra we had met, in the hotel, Dr. Partridge, Brigade-Surgeon, who has a beautiful villa—Bella Vista—on Cumballa Hill, and who is actively engaged in missionary work during his spare hours. Like a good Samaritan and Christian as well, he had compassion on us in the dirty, dilapidated, mosquito-infected Adelphi Hotel, and insisted on our removing to his house on Monday, where we spent, fanned by the delightful northern breeze, our last days in India.

He took us in the afternoon to visit a Parsee house, in which reside seven sons and three daughters, all married, having, one of the ladies said, "dozens upon dozens" of children, and rejoicing in wonderful barrel-organs. Then there were dinner and luncheon parties, a ball given by the bachelors of Bombay in a fine native house at Malabar Point, horse-races at Byculla, and a variety of other engagements and amusements for old and young. I counted eighteen cotton factories from the balcony of the spacious Byculla Club.

The day before leaving I paid a visit to the Free Church Mission Establishment, where Dr Wilson so long laboured, and where 500 scholars are now being taught; lunched with the Governor in the Secretariat, went off to see the *Jumna* transport, and then drove round Malabar and Cumballa Hills. Some parts of the former, with its villas and flowers, remind me of Mustapha at Algiers. The latter has the purer, fresher air, and will surely become the favourite suburb of Bombay. Warden Road, leading along the sea to Breach Candy, is the paradise of nurserymen and maids in the evening.

CHAPTER XIV.

DEPARTURE FROM INDIA.

HOW charming was our last night in India! The moon shone through the palm-trees upon the spacious balcony of Bella Vista; and we felt a sort of melancholy steal over us as we thought of the kind friends from whom we were to part—a dear daughter whom we might not see again for years, and a country to which we were about to say good-bye for ever. The sea-breeze sighed among the branches, and the waves of the Indian Ocean, breaking gently on the rocks, were our lullaby.

As the clock struck five on Thursday afternoon, 23rd February, the *Venetia's* anchor was raised; and before we sat down to dinner I had my last look of India. The north-east monsoon was blowing, and for thirty-six hours the ship rolled a good deal; but by Saturday morning the wind died away, and at noon that day we had run 309 miles—quite a feat for a P. and O.

I have read "Twenty-one Days in India; or, the Tour of Sir Ali Baba, K.C.B.," by the late lamented Mr. Mackay. It is very clever, and many truths are told in its witty, satirical sketches. Here is what he says of ritualistic clergymen :—"In a heathen country their paltry fetishism and incomprehensible technicalities are peculiarly offensive and injurious to the interests of civilisation and Christianity." About the Rajahs he remarks :—"They have built their houses of cards on the thin crust of British Rule that now covers the crater, and they are ever ready to pour a pannikin of water into a crack to quench the explosive forces rumbling below." Of the poor ryot he writes:—"Famine is the horizon of the Indian villager; insufficient food is the foreground." Then follows a beautiful description of the fertile soil and glorious climate, and he concludes:—"Amid this easeful and luscious splendour the villager labours and starves."

I have spent some time in looking over back numbers of "The Quarterly Journal of the Poona Sabha." The following extracts faithfully represent the sentiments of every educated native whom I met regarding the past and present administrations:—

"The four years of Lord Lytton's administration of India have proved disastrous beyond all precedent to the true interests of the millions committed to his fostering care. The besetting sin of his administration has been that it was eminently untruthful, repressive and reactionary at home, unjustly aggressive abroad, and disastrous to the safety of our finance and material prosperity."

"We cannot but congratulate both India and England on the overthrow of an administration which has been without a parallel in the annals of British India for its disastrous failure in war, in finance, in legislation and administration."

"We can only hope that with the retirement of Sir R. Temple, and the enforced resignation of Lord Lytton and Sir John Strachey, the retrograde and blustering policy which overshadowed all the departments of administration, and repressed the growth of our national aspirations, may be said to have had its fitting close, and that a more genuinely liberal, just, and sympathetic rule will dawn upon the country, and undo the disastrous work of a false and short-lived Imperialism."

"Under these circumstances, we are gratefully thankful that our rulers feel disposed to review their Indian policy, and to reorganise their system of Indian government. The old policy of blustering, and of assuming imperial airs, and of devising plans to humiliate and weaken the natives of India, and of excluding them from all consideration as if they were 'dumb driven cattle,' has now been wisely abandoned. The time has come when the shackles of India should be relaxed, and when the natives should be taken into confidence, when their proposals for conserving and improving their commercial and political condition should be carefully considered, when their aristocracy, which necessarily and naturally leads them, should be respected, and when the police arrangements and the municipal and local Government of India should be placed on a better footing. India has now learnt to look about herself, to examine, to improve, and to aspire. With the accession of the Liberals into power, and the deputation of Lord Ripon and Major Baring to control the destinies of this country, the dawn of a better order of things has filled the land with hopefulness, and dispersed the gloom of war and humiliation."

Those interested in the extension of the principle of representation should read the two extracts subjoined:—

"Your petitioners submit that the time has come when the views of the independent native and European public should find a recognised place; and the only way in which this end can be secured is to admit a few representative members elected by the leading cities and populous centres throughout the country. The representative principle has now found place in the municipalities of the three Presidency towns, and has worked satisfactorily. This principle might be safely extended to the other large centres of population, and the municipalities so elected might be safely trusted to send representative men to the several legislatures. These members might not find a place in the executive Government for the present, but if the right of interpellating the executive officers upon all questions of public importance were allowed to them, the check against arbitrary rule will be effective, and the criticism based upon such information in the press and in public petitions will cease to be non-effective as at present —thus establishing greater harmony than has obtained hitherto by allowing Government to justify its measures to the people. The present advanced state of public intelligence in this country justifies the extension of this right, as, without the adequate check it will provide, all further progress will be greatly retarded."

"The real struggle will have to be fought out in India, and it is in the enlargement of the Indian Legislative Councils that all our hope for a better future is centred. Mr. Digby proposes to have a council consisting of the ex-officio executive councillors, supplemented by the addition of the ex-officio collectors, and a due proportion of nominated and elected European and native members. We do not approve of the suggestion regarding the ex-officio collectors. The District Local Fund Committees, enlarged and liberalised under the new decentralisation schemes, will be in a position to send their representatives to the council. This will supply the Conservative element, and the Liberal element will be effectively supplied by the representatives of the large city municipalities. These two elements, with a due admixture of the ex-officio and nominated members, will be for a long time to come a sufficient representation of all interests."

I had the happiness to be in at the death of the Vernacular Press Act. The following quotations express accurately the views not only of natives but of many Englishmen who spoke to me on the subject:—

"But in what light can their conduct be viewed if they wilfully increase the difficulty of knowing what the people think and feel about their intentions and doings a thousand-fold; if instead of trying to make themselves acquainted with what passes in the innermost recesses of the minds of the subjects, they designedly throw a veil over them, as if a knowledge of the disease is not the first condition of its cure, and as if the task of the physician will be smoothed by ignoring its symptoms. Can good government be ensured to the people without the rulers being acquainted with their modes of thinking and feeling, with what they consider as their grievances, with the impressions they receive from the acts of Government officials, with their habits and opinions and sentiments and prejudices? Can this desirable information be had independently of the native press? Certainly not, if we are to believe Lord William Bentinck, one of the most successful and really philanthropic rulers of India, who is reported to have said 'That he had derived more information from the Indian press than from all the councils, all the boards, and all the secretaries by whom he was surrounded.' Can a fettered press venture to supply freely to Government any information regarding its officials and the people which it needs for successfully conducting the administration of the country? Who can, with the sword of Damocles hanging over his head, freely denounce the conduct and doings of government officials, when the latter are so prone to resent any sort of criticism of their acts as an insult offered to the majesty of Great Britain, and to confound it with an attempt at sapping the foundation of the British Empire in India?"

"The Act for the better control of oriental publications was passed by the late Government three years ago, under an apprehension of political necessity which subsequent events have not, by the admission of all parties, justified. The official papers since published have shown that there was not that concensus of opinions even in the most responsible advisers of Government which alone could have warranted the wide departure from the acknowledged policy of the Government in this connection, sanctioned as it was by nearly fifty years' experience of the great benefits which had resulted from the unrestricted liberty of the press in this country. The only precedent for such action was that afforded by a measure adopted by Lord Canning under the excitement of the troubles caused by the Mutiny of 1857; but Lord Canning's measure was free from any invidious distinction between vernacular and English publications, and it was only temporary in its application. The present measure was apparently passed in great hurry, in view of apprehended troubles in Russia. That justification has long since ceased, and the measure had been practically inoperative, except in a few isolated cases where the action of local governments has had to be controlled and set aside by the interference of His Excellency the Viceroy in Council. This Sabha has from the first protested against the enactment of such a measure and its retention on the statute book, on the grounds that it cast an undeserved suspicion upon the loyalty of the vernacular newspapers, that it prevented the free discussion of official measures which, under the circumstances of an alien rule like that which obtains in British India, is so necessary in the interests both of the governed and the governing classes, that it checked from the sense of ignoble fear the growth of a healthy public opinion, and that it invested petty local authorities with a power of vexatious interference which cannot fail to demoralise them."

The excuse for passing this measure was that many of these newspapers evinced a bad spirit, and attacked the Government in improper words. If this test were applied to not a few of the English periodicals published in India it would go hard with them.

Until I visited the country I had no idea that there existed in our Empire journals so replete with vulgar vituperation as the Jingo newspapers of Hindostan. I read in one of them a leader on Lord Hartington, putting into his mouth words which he never used, and imputing to him opinions which I know he does not hold, and then showering upon him names worthy only of Billingsgate. Several men of influence expressed themselves to me thoroughly ashamed of a portion of their press; and remarked that if the vernacular papers were violent, they had had a very evil example set them by the organs of the officials who were the authors of the Act now happily repealed.

A writer in one of the numbers of the *Poona Sabha Journal* discusses the policy of retaining the armies of the native states; and I give his arguments against disbandment, although not agreeing with him, and taking care to remark that no one advocates forcible measures in bringing about a change of system.

"1. The native armies in all the larger states distinctly rest on treaty obligations which are binding upon the paramount power, which has repeatedly admitted the force of these obligations. Such obligations cannot be dissolved without the free and mutual consent of both parties.

"2. This appanage is the last privilege left to the royal houses. Measures of forcible disbandment cannot but cause dissatisfaction among the native states.

"3. The armies are not a source of danger to the British Government. Their strength and numbers are overrated. Badly armed, badly officered, badly disciplined, and wholly disunited, they have no power for mischief.

"4. They are, at the same time, very useful auxiliaries, especially as against Asiatic powers on the frontiers of our provinces, in respect of whom the use of the regular British army involves a needless waste of money and strength.

"5. They have rendered important services in the early wars, as also in the Mutiny struggle, and have proved valuable auxiliaries in the present Afghan war.

"6. Their loyalty and insignificance renders jealous watchfulness unnecessary, and if more confidence were placed in them, they would render a considerable reduction of the British garrison possible.

"7. They are beyond all comparison a cheap agency, and good material to rely upon as a recruiting-ground for the British Indian forces.

"8. The whole population being disarmed and demartialised, the native armies are the only available militia and reserve force to fall back upon.

"9. The native British Indian force is *par excellence* a mercenary body. The sepoys require to be counterbalanced by these native armies, which are for the most part national and not mercenary, and which, at all events, will never make common cause with the sepoys.

"10. In the present state of India, when the whole of Central Asia may be expected with Russian help and propulsion any day to come down upon us, it is not safe to trust to the single support of the regular British Indian forces alone. There should be many small centres and foci of dependent authority, scattered over the country, with their opportunities of education in military habits, and in the higher art of leading and controlling men.

"11. In many native states society rests on a feudal or military basis. This state of things cannot be disturbed without affecting the integrity of the states. The Sirdars and military classes, for whom British India offers no field, are usefully provided for in these native armies.

"12. The purposes sought to be accomplished by

forcible disbandment can be equally well achieved by a policy of greater trust and confidence. If the armies of native states are badly armed and officered and disciplined, these defects may be removed by the help of British officers lent to these states to effect these reforms, and improve the race of native officers."

CHAPTER XV.

ON THE INDIAN OCEAN.

THIS voyaging on the Indian Ocean is the perfection of travelling. The sea is so calm, the sun so bright, the air so balmy.

When I rose on Wednesday morning we were in sight of the rock of Aden, and at 10 o'clock we anchored in the harbour. There was a delightfully refreshing southern breeze blowing, and we landed to explore the place, driving in light covered carriages to the town on the opposite side of the peninsula from the landing-place, to the celebrated tanks, which hold millions of gallons of water, through two tunnels to the cantonment of the English troops and the lines facing Arabia, and to the pier, where native craft land provisions and fuel. What a grim, arid, sepulchral-looking place it is! The little one-barrel water-carts drawn by camels, the profusely-ornamented women, the number of vehicles of all kinds on the roads, the total absence of trees—indeed, of all vegetation except in the small irrigated garden at the tanks—and the sharp outlines of the peaks strike you. Then the harbour is always full of vessels — steamers coming and going continually: a Russian man-of-war entered when we were at anchor, saluted, and her salute was returned from a battery on the shore.

Brigadier-General Blair, V.C., was our fellow-passenger from Bombay, on his way to assume the governorship of Aden for five years — a brave soldier and most agreeable companion, to whom we wish health and happiness during his residence on that shadeless rock.

As 4 p.m. struck we weighed anchor, and had rather a rough time of it in the night, the scuttles being closed. When I got on deck at 7 a.m. all the square sails were set, and we were running past the Island of Gebel Zukur, with the wrecks of the *Duke of Lancaster* and *Penguin* on the port bow. Gradually the wind increased, until at noon our good ship began to take in seas; and not until we had passed the Twelve Apostles did the turmoil end.

The *Venetia* is a very substantial and excellent sea-boat, built and engined by Denny of Dumbarton, 2,726 tons, and commanded by Captain Daniell, who spared no effort to make everyone happy and comfortable on board.

Travellers in India and in the steamers to and fro will be struck with the frequent discussions which they hear about the taxation of that country. There can be no doubt that the wealthier classes there do not bear their fair share. In fact, the rich natives get off nearly scot-free, and millionaires not in trade need pay no more than the ryot whose salt is so heavily burdened.* Even the landed proprietor is charged a mere trifle in comparison with what his forefathers paid under the settlements of Akbar; and the poorer classes will

* "The exemption of the richer classes from taxation is a political mistake, which, as time goes on, and knowledge and intelligence increase, must become more and more mischievous:"—"India," by Sir J. and General Strachey.

"It is notorious that the mercantile wealth of the country, which is considerable, and daily increasing, pays very little, in proportion to its means, for the protection and advantages which it enjoys under British rule:"—Mr. Bazett Colvin on "Indian Taxation.

always have a grievance as long as no income-tax, or similar mode of reaching the large number of wealthy natives, is imposed.

Well-paid civil servants and baboos unite against any such proposal, their newspapers enlarging on the difficulty of getting it to work fairly, especially in a country like India, where deceit is a science. Yet I have met British officials who believe that with a little courage and determination on the part of the authorities it might be imposed with safety, would remove a great injustice, and prove a national benefit. But while rich people pay a mere trifle towards the expenses of government, the small holders and labourers do contribute a considerable portion of their hard earnings in the shape of a salt tax; and instead of reiterating impressions of my own regarding their impoverished condition, let me quote two passages from "British India and its Rulers," just published by Judge Cunningham, of the High Court of Calcutta:—

"On the whole it may be said that the great mass of the occupants of the soil of India must be, from the smallness of their holdings, and the numbers who have to be supported on them, at the best of times hard pressed for the means of subsistence ; that, in the case of a very large number in Bengal and upper India, the hardships of their position are enhanced by the presence of a class of more or less exacting landlords, whose eagerness for an increased rental is favoured by the increased necessity of a growing population to find room on the soil ; that habits of improvidence, and traditional customs of occasional extravagance, not unfrequently destroy any chance there might be of a rise to greater comfort and security ; that the almost universal practice of dependence on money-lenders has of late years entailed more serious consequences, owing partly to the larger and more assured interest in the soil which the landowner enjoys under the British revenue settlement, and the better credit he thus obtains ; and partly to the speedier, more exact, and more effectual procedure of the civil courts ; that some of the conditions of modern life may have tended to enhance the difficulties of particular classes ; that though there can be no doubt that a large amount of wealth is being brought into the country, the increase of population, which is likely to be accelerated, will, in years to come, make a large demand on the resources so created ; and that, as no considerable outlets, other than in agricultural employment, at present exist, the pressure on the soil and the penury of the less thrifty and capable agriculturists, is likely, in the absence of some new form of relief, to become still severer than at present."

"The grave political and social dangers to which an impoverished, degraded, and rack-rented peasantry gives rise, are assuming every year a more menacing aspect, and the controversy has a tendency, as the pressure of the population on the soil increases, to become continually more embittered. Official evidence of the weightiest character, and tendered from the most various quarters, makes it impossible to doubt that the condition of the tenantry in several parts of India is a peril to society, and a disgrace to any civilised administration."

The following from the same book, in regard to local self-government, is especially interesting at a time when that subject is much discussed at home:—

"It was resolved accordingly to entrust to the local governments certain important departments of the administration, to hand over to them certain specified funds for the purpose of meeting the expenditure thus involved and to hold them responsible for obtaining, either by economies, rearrangement, or, if necessary, local taxation, the means for defraying any outlay beyond that covered by the allotment. Cost of jails, registration, police, education, medical services, printing, roads, and some other items, were thus handed over to the several provincial administrations, a corresponding allotment of revenue being made to each.

"The gross sum made over for these services was about four-and-a-half millions; this has subsequently been increased by the further development of the system to five-and-a-half millions, and the Government is gradually extending it, as opportunities offer, in various parts of the Empire.

"Bengal is now responsible for all civil expenditure, except that on opium, and for all loss on its productive public works. It has the benefit of all branches of income except land revenue, opium, and salt. The success of the scheme in this province has been so marked that Bengal has already been able to make a material contribution to the Imperial revenue from the large margin of profit which accrued to her under the arrangement. Similar measures will hereafter be carried out elsewhere.

"All authorities concur in attesting the excellent results of these measures as regards economy and activity in the local administrations. The continuous growth in local expenditure has been successfully arrested ; every branch of the provincial administrations has received a wholesome stimulus towards care in the use of public funds ; the local goverments have been relieved from a minute financial control which was a constant source of irritation, and the Government of India from duties of supervision which threatened to overwhelm it. The next few years will, it may be hoped, witness the development of a scheme whose substantial success is already beyond dispute."

I add a couple more passages in regard to the all-important land question :—

"In the majority of instances the landlords are now purely rent-receivers, doing nothing for the land, and spending none of the rental on the improvement of the soil. On the other hand, by the invasion of the occupants' rights, and the reduction of large classes to the level of poverty-stricken and rack-rented tenants-at-will, the land-owners have presented a formidable obstacle to the gradual improvements which cultivators with secure tenure and an interest in the soil would have been certain to effect. A tenantry in the condition of the Behar ryot, holding on a precarious tenure under great proprietors and "contractors," whose one interest it is to force up the rents, is the best guarantee for improvident, wasteful tillage and an exhausted soil."

"In Bengal, and especially Behar, the landlord system has had the longest and completest trial, and the result of unrestricted competition for the land has been most clearly illustrated. We have now, after a century's experience, to deal with a question which, difficult at the outset, has become, with each year's fresh accretion or interests, prejudices, and customs, less easy of solution, and which is now so entangled in conflicting claims that its adjustment can scarcely be effected without bitter heart-burnings, class animosities, accusations of bad faith, and all the other inevitable ill-results of a too long postponed reform. Reform, however, is admitted, even by those who are most alive to its difficulties, to be indispensable. Its successful accomplishment would be the crowning feat of Indian statesmanship."

Everyone who cares to know about India should read Mr. Cunningham's book, although in the judgment of men who have spent a lifetime in the country, it is written in too *couleur de rose* a style, and although nothing is said of the "gulf gradually widening" (some observers of long experience assure me,) between the educated natives and their rulers, nothing of the demand for an extension of representation, nothing of the complaints recorded by me in preceding pages. The information given is, however, accurate and well put together, and everyone must regard it as a valuable contribution to our knowledge of India. The annual average foreign trade of that country, the author tells us, has increased from 18·6 millions in 1834-39 to 122,000,000 in 1879-80, and the yearly export of tea now amounts to 34,000,000 pounds of the value of £3,000,000 sterling.

According to the most recent official accounts to which I have had access—viz., those of 1879, there are 1,363 tea gardens in our Indian dominions, having an out-turn of 44,771,632 lbs., and a capital invested in them of £88,794,298, and paying an average interest of 9·47 per cent.

We had a calm, cool Friday, another breeze succeeded, and by 3.0 a.m. on Sunday we were abreast the Dædalus light; we passed the remarkable and dangerous coral rocks called "The Brothers" at noon, had a rough night, and found that next morning we were in a different climate—everyone was shivering, and preferring the sunny side of the ship as she ran along that dreadfully desolate coast.

CHAPTER XVI.

THE SUEZ CANAL—HOME.

AT 10.30 on Monday morning, 6th March, our anchor was dropped in the roadstead of Suez, among numerous steamers of various nations, including H.M.S. *Cleopatra*, and the *Khedive*, and *Teheran* of the P. & O. Line. Then followed the usual absurd ceremonies of the quarantine system—a health-despatch received on a forked stick, a list of passengers thrown into a tin box, and the mails put in tarred sacks, Bombay and Aden being infected ports, and passengers from the *Venetia* not being allowed to land in order to proceed to Alexandria by rail.

I have mentioned previously that the British Government in India no longer manage idol temples, but we adopted the endowments which existed before our rule, and now pay very large sums to the Hindoo and Mahommedan places of worship, in the shape of annual cash payments; and, besides, lands and villages are assigned for their support to an extent the value of which it is not easy accurately to discover. In the Bombay Presidency alone, and excluding five districts not in the returns, 2,725 district religious establishments, and 11,039 village temples, are paid no less than 214,947r.; and the total sum contributed, taking cash payments and assignments together, is computed to be five lacs of rupees. In Madras the return of November, 1872, shows that land revenue alienations equal to 2,332,570r. in the case of Hindoos, and 263,194r. in the case of Mahommedans, are applied for religious purposes, while 525,407r. were disbursed from treasuries for the same uses.

Sooner or later the Government must face the question how this system can be put an end to, and these payments be made to cease, leaving the temples and mosques ultimately, as a writer in one of the journals puts it, "to depend entirely on the votive offerings of the people." Of course this is a difficult and delicate question, not to be settled off-hand, in a day or a year, but its discussion and eventual decision cannot be avoided, and the ostrich-like policy of refusing to look at it at all, will in the long run be found to be inadmissible. In order, however, to deal with it without fear, we ourselves must be without reproach, and my enquiries in India strongly confirm my previous impression that our ecclesiastical system and establishment of chaplains there cannot be defended.

As it may be necessary for me elsewhere to treat this subject at some length, and in detail, I only observe here that a large number of our so-called chaplains do not preach to soldiers, or even civil servants, but to planters and merchants who ought to pay for their own clergymen; that influential deputations of Hindoos, Mahommedans, and Christians waited upon me in Calcutta, Madras, and Poona, and in many other places gentlemen privately urged me to bring parliamentary pressure to bear against the system of paying bishops and priests of the Established Church of England, and clergymen of the churches of Scotland and Rome, out of revenue principally derived from persons who are not

Christians; that chaplains, considering themselves a superior class on account of their official position, are often found at variance with the more experienced and hard-working missionaries; that many earnest Christians in India told me that it would be better even for the soldiers if the State did not interfere at all; that the ritualistic practices now so prevalent among the class are doing serious damage to the progress of Christianity; and that the devices fallen upon to get men, who really do no military duty, placed on the ecclesiastical and State-paid staff, are discreditable to the congregations who thus save their money, injurious to Christianity, and contrary to the spirit of the Queen's Proclamation.

No further step can be taken about heathen temples until Government sets its house in order in this respect; and I earnestly hope that they will not be content with paltry reductions and more stringent new rules, but boldly recognising the justice of the complaints, as boldly apply the axe to the root of the tree. No one ever expressed to me an opinion that there is any objection on *principle* to chaplains for *soldiers* being paid out of revenue, although several persons well acquainted with the subject did say that they believed that the spiritual wants of the military would be better supplied if there were no State clergymen at all. A leaf should be taken out of the Ceylon book. In that island a time has been fixed when all such payments by Government shall cease, and the congregations connected with the richest of the Christian churches, on its termination, be given an opportunity of doing what has been already done by the poorer sects—viz., supporting their own clergymen.

We are now waiting our turn to get into the Suez Canal. Here are the most recent statistics in regard to that remarkable work, in favour of which I voted in the House of Commons many years ago, when we were in a small minority, because opposed by the engineering talent and supposed statesmanship of Great Britain. It was opened in 1869. In 1870 there passed through it 496 vessels, with a gross tonnage of 486,000, which paid 5,159,357 francs in toll. In 1881 these figures had risen to 2,727 ships, 5,794,401 tons, and 51,274,352 francs; and during last year the number of vessels that passed through exceeded 3,000. Of the 2,727 vessels in 1881, 2,251 were British; in 1870, 64 per cent of the tonnage belonged to Great Britain; in 1881 that per-centage had risen to 83, and it is still rising. From its opening up to the end of May 1882, 18,634 steamers have passed through the Canal; of this number 14,159 were British, and the French come next with 1,048 only. The receipts during the years 1870 to 1881 inclusive amounted to very nearly thirteen millions sterling, the average toll per ship being about £750, and the net profits are now reported to amount to 14 or 15 per cent. per annum. Shades of Robert Stephenson and Lord Palmerston!

By some inexplicable arrangement we were detained at Suez all day, and not allowed to enter the canal until next morning, although a Dutch steamer which arrived two hours after us went in before sunset; and when morning came a dense and very cold fog prevented us weighing anchor until 8.30, and then at 10.30 we were stopped for five hours in a siding until eight steamers—all British—passed on towards Suez.

We spent the night at anchor in the Bitter Lakes, and a short distance from Ismailia, at the entrance of Lake Timsah, found the merchant-steamer *Lisgard* aground, and blocking up the channel; so we had to lie there for twenty-one hours, until she had been lightened of sufficient cargo to enable her to float. That operation might have been performed much quicker, but the quarantine regulations did not permit of assistance from the shore. Everyone believes that this farcical system has been adopted at the instance of the owners of steam-launches, as all steamers in quarantine are obliged to have a steam-launch before them, for which the charge is twenty-five francs an hour—a direct premium on delay—the presence of a pilot on board the supposed infected ship being inadmissible. Of course a continuance or renewal of this preposterous restriction on trade, and enormous loss to shipowners and inconvenience to passengers, cannot be tolerated much longer. The whole proceedings of the so-called sanitary commission require being looked into.

The mirage was very remarkable between Ismailia and Port Said, the mounds in the desert appearing like islands in the sea.

We were booked for the *Khedive* to Malta, but found she had sailed the night before, and as soon as the *Venetia* dropped anchor we were transferred to the *Teheran*, from Calcutta. All Friday and Saturday it blew from the north-west, and as it had evidently been blowing heavier a day or two before there was a considerable sea on, and we had rather a poor time of it; but Sunday dawned fair and fine, with a calm sea, and we reached Malta, which I had not seen for thirty-three years, early on Monday morning. The great increase of population, especially around Valetta, and even in the formerly deserted region of St. Paul's Bay struck me, and I observed with regret as many priests and their consequential beggars as before.

Our quickest way home was by the French steamer which carries the British mails to Syracuse, thence by rail to Messina—one of the most beautiful routes in Europe—the mountain, rock, sea-cliff, and valley scenery varying in loveliness every few minutes, and majestic, solemn Etna presiding over all; and so on to Naples by steamer again.

There I read a synopsis of the Indian Budget, and was overjoyed to find it in every particular in accordance with the opinions which I had formed. It reflects the highest credit on the statesmanship of Lord Ripon and Major Baring; especially are they deserving of praise for reducing the salt-tax, notwithstanding the opposition of the monied classes—native and European—who think too much of themselves and too little of the poor.*

I have since had an opportunity of perusing the East India financial statement as presented to Parliament in a blue book, and recommend

* "When the time comes for reducing taxation we should begin with the taxes on salt and clothing, which add to the cost of the necessaries of life." "Further reductions in the salt duties are, on all grounds, desirable, both for the benefit of the people and of the finances." "Indian Finance," by Sir J. and Maj. Gen. Strachey.

all who are interested in the social well-being of our great dependency to study it with care. Anything more admirable has seldom been laid before the House of Commons. The following from paragraph 34 will give great satisfaction to all who conversed with me on the subject:—

> "It is the intention of Her Majesty's Government, and of the Government of India, that a constantly increasing share of the work of the country shall be performed by natives of India. Not only will this gradual change add to the ties which already bind educated natives and the chief native families to the British Government, but the work will be performed more economically than hitherto. The number of native gentlemen holding offices of trust and position has increased during the last three years, and will continue to do so under the combined influence of the annual admissions to the Covenanted Civil Service in both England and India, and the rules of 1879, regarding appointments to the Uncovenanted Service."

Paragraph 58 bears out what is stated in the foregoing pages, regarding the poverty of the people in certain districts:—

> "A careful examination of the economic condition of the people in the various provinces of India leads to the conclusion that in the North-Western Provinces and

Oudh there are but slight signs of any improvement in the mass of the people during the last decade. The number of people with incomes of not less than Rs. 500 a year, derived from trade, and assessed to the License Tax in 1880-81, was 1,550 less than the number assessed to the Income Tax in 1870-71 and 1871-72. This would seem to indicate a diminution of the trade-wealth of these Provinces. On the whole, it may be said that nowhere in India is a reduction of taxation more required than in the North-Western Provinces and Oudh."

I give an extract from paragraph 65, which shows that the Government are fully alive to one of the great questions of the day:—

"Boards and committees for the administration of certain local funds already exist in most parts of India. We now wish to widen the sphere of action hitherto assigned to these bodies. The Provincial Governments have, therefore, been invited to hand over to them such items of revenue and expenditure as may appear most suited to give them a real interest in the administration of the resources at their command, and, on the other hand, to take over as a provincial charge some items of expenditure, such as police, over which local bodies cannot exercise any real control. I will not, however, at present discuss this question at length. The Local Governments have been consulted upon the subject, and until their answers are received it will be impossible to decide upon the particular measures which it may eventually be deemed desirable to adopt. I will only say, that whilst we recognise that the development of local self-government must be gradual, and not of a nature to outstrip the wants of the country and the standard of political education at which the people have arrived, at the same time we are desirous of making a real step in advance in the proposed direction."

Paragraph 173 should be studied by those who, in their anxiety to benefit the Chinese, do not sufficiently take into consideration what would be the effect of any sudden change in the opium duties at the present time on the poorer classes in India:—

"From the language which is occasionally used on this subject in England, I am led to infer that many influential persons, animated by a laudable zeal to benefit the population of China, are perhaps somewhat forgetful of the duty we owe to the population of India. It has been calculated that the average income per head of population in India is not more than Rs. 27 a year; and although I am not prepared to pledge myself to the accuracy of a calculation of this sort, it is sufficiently accurate to justify the conclusion that the tax-paying community is exceedingly poor. To derive any very large increase of revenue from so poor a population as this is obviously impossible, and if it were possible would be unjustifiable. Apart from the practical issues involved, there are, indeed, two aspects of the question from the point of view of public morality. If, on the one hand, it be urged that it is immoral to obtain a revenue from the use of opium amongst a section of the Chinese community, on the other hand it may replied that to tax the poorest classes in India in order to benefit China would be a cruel injustice ; and it is to be remembered that no large increase of revenue in India is possible, unless by means of a tax which will affect those classes. To tax India in order to provide a cure, which would almost certainly be ineffectual, to the vices of the Chinese, would be wholly unjustifiable."

At Paris I received the following letter from one of the ablest, most zealous, and most experienced of India's civil servants :—

"I must write a line to say how sorry I was not to see you again before you left India. The native press and public are unanimous in expressing gratitude to you for the patient and sympathetic hearing you have given them. All they ask for is independent and impartial enquiry, and they are confident that they will then prove the correctness of their statements and the moderation of their demands. It is a striking feature of the controversy between the Indian official and non-official world, that when unprejudiced and qualified judges, like yourself and Mr. Caird, come to this country, the official organs are so very angry with them for the opinions they form. The fact is, that a large proportion of officials, even during a long service, remain quite isolated and profoundly ignorant of the facts and feelings around them ; and an intelligent outside observer, who mixes freely with the natives, will learn more in a few weeks of the *true* state of the country than is known to them."

It will be a great satisfaction to me if anything in the preceding pages should induce other family parties to follow our example, and give themselves a delightful holiday by spending "A Winter in India."

THE END.

CASSELL, PETTER, GALPIN & CO., Belle Sauvage Works, London, E.C.

SELECTIONS FROM VOLUMES

Published by Cassell, Petter, Galpin & Co.

NEW LIFE OF CROMWELL.

Oliver Cromwell: the Man and his Mission. By J. ALLANSON PICTON. With Steel Portrait. Price 7s. 6d.

A Winter in India. By the Right Hon. W. E. BAXTER, M.P. Illustrated. Crown 8vo, cloth, 5s.

Wealth Creation. By AUGUSTUS MONGREDIEN. Crown 8vo, cloth, price 5s.

Constitutional History and Political Development of the United States. By SIMON STERNE, of the New York Bar. 5s.

The History of the Year. A Complete Narrative of the Events of the Past Year. Crown 8vo, cloth, 6s.

England: its People, Polity, and Pursuits. By T. H. S. ESCOTT. *Cheap Edition*, in One Vol., price 7s. 6d.

A History of Modern Europe. By C. A. FYFFE, M.A., Fellow of University College, Oxford. Vols. I. and II., demy 8vo, 12s. each.

Wood Magic: A Fable. By RICHARD JEFFERIES, Author of "The Gamekeeper at Home," &c. *Cheap Edition*, cloth, 6s.

English and Irish Land Questions. Collected Essays by the Right Hon. G. SHAW-LEFEVRE, M.P., First Commissioner of Works and Public Buildings. Price 6s.

A Police Code, and Manual of the Criminal Law. By C. E. HOWARD VINCENT, Director of Criminal Investigations. Cloth, price 6s. *Pocket Edition*, for Policemen and Householders, with an Address to Constables by Mr. Justice HAWKINS, 2s.

The Landed Interest and the Supply of Food. By Sir JAMES CAIRD, K.C.B., F.R.S. *New and Enlarged Edition.* Cloth, 5s.

A Ride to Khiva. By Lieut.-Col. FRED BURNABY. *Cheap Edition*, 3s. 6d.; *People's Edition*, 6d.

The Life of the Right Hon. W. E. Gladstone. By GEORGE BARNETT SMITH. With Two Steel Portraits. *Cheap Edition*, in One Vol., cloth, 5s. *Jubilee Edition*, 1s.

Russia. By D. MACKENZIE WALLACE, M.A. *Cheap Edition*, in One Vol., with Two Maps, 10s. 6d.

Cassell, Petter, Galpin & Co.: Ludgate Hill, London; Paris; and New York.

5 R—1082

The British Army. From the Restoration to the Revolution. By Sir SIBBALD SCOTT, Bart. Demy 8vo, cloth, 21s.

Remedies for War, Political and Legal. By Prof. SHELDON AMOS, M.A., Barrister-at-Law. Price 6s.

Universal History, Cassell's Illustrated. Vol. I. With numerous High-class Engravings. Price 9s.

Gleanings from Popular Authors. Vol. I. With Original Illustrations. Price 9s.

England, Cassell's History of. With about 2,000 Illustrations. Nine Vols., cloth, 9s. each; or in library binding, £4 10s.

United States, Cassell's History of the. With 600 Illustrations and Maps. 1,950 pages, extra crown 4to. Complete in Three Vols., cloth, £1 7s.; or in library binding, £1 10s.

India, Cassell's History of. With about 400 Maps, Plans, and Illustrations. Extra crown 4to, Two Vols., cloth, 18s.; or in library binding, £1.

The Russo-Turkish War, Cassell's History of. Complete in Two Vols. With about 500 Illustrations. 9s. each.

British Battles on Land and Sea. By JAMES GRANT. With about 600 Illustrations. Three Vols., cloth, £1 7s.; or in library binding, £1 10s.

Old and New London. A Narrative of its History, its People, and its Places. With 1,200 Illustrations. Complete in Six Vols., 9s. each; or in library binding, £3.

Heroes of Britain in Peace and War. By E. HODDER. With 300 Illustrations. Two Vols., 7s. 6d. each. Library binding, One Vol., price 12s. 6d.

Decisive Events in History. *Fifth Edition.* With Full-page Original Illustrations. Cloth gilt, 5s.

Through the Light Continent; or, The United States in 1877-8. By WILLIAM SAUNDERS. 10s. 6d.

The History of Protestantism. By the Rev. J. A. WYLIE, LL.D. With 600 Original Illustrations. Three Vols., 4to, cloth, £1 7s.; or in library binding, £1 10s.

Cassell, Petter Galpin & Co.: Ludgate Hill, London; Paris; and New York.

The Magazine of Art. Volume V. With about 400 Illustrations by the first Artists of the day, and beautifully-executed Etching, for Frontispiece. Cloth gilt, gilt edges, 16s. *The price of Vols. I., II., III., and IV. has been increased—Vols. I. and IV. to 21s. each, Vols. II. and III. to 15s. each.*

Evangeline. *Edition de Luxe.* With magnificent Original Illustrations by FRANK DICKSEE, A.R.A., beautifully reproduced in Photogravure. *** *Further particulars, with price, &c., may be obtained of any Bookseller.*

Longfellow's Poetical Works. With Original Engravings by the best English, American, and Continental Artists. Royal 4to, £3 3s.

Picturesque Europe. *Popular Edition.* Vol. I., with 13 exquisite Steel Plates, and about 200 Original Engravings by the best Artists. Cloth gilt, 18s. N.B.—The *Original Edition*, in Five magnificent Volumes, royal 4to size, can still be obtained, price £10 10s.

Egypt: Descriptive, Historical, and Picturesque. By Prof. G. EBERS. Translated by CLARA BELL, with Notes by SAMUEL BIRCH, LL.D., D.C.L., F.S.A. With Original magnificent Engravings. Cloth bevelled, gilt edges. Vol. I., £2 5s.; Vol. II., £2 12s. 6d.

Picturesque America. Vol. I., with 12 exquisite Steel Plates and about 200 Original Wood Engravings. Royal 4to, £2 2s.

Landscape Painting in Oils, A Course of Lessons in. By A. F. GRACE, Turner Medallist, Royal Academy. With Nine Reproductions in Colour. Extra demy folio, cloth, gilt edges, 42s.

Illustrated British Ballads. With Several Hundred Original Illustrations by some of the first Artists of the day. Complete in Two Vols. Cloth, gilt edges, 21s.

Character Sketches from Dickens. Large Drawings by FRED BARNARD of Sidney Carton, Mr. Pickwick, Alfred Jingle, Little Dorrit, Mrs. Gamp, and Bill Sikes. In Portfolio, imperial 4to, 5s. the set.

Pictures of Bird Life in Pen and Pencil. With Illustrations by GIACOMELLI. Imperial 4to, 21s.

The Changing Year. Being Poems and Pictures of Life and Nature. With Illustrations. Cloth gilt, 7s. 6d.

The Doré Fine Art Volumes comprise—

	£ s. d.		£ s. d.
Milton's Paradise Lost	1 1 0	**La Fontaine's Fables**	1 10 0
The Doré Gallery	5 5 0	**Don Quixote**	0 15 0
The Doré Bible	4 4 0	**Munchausen**	0 5 0
Dante's Inferno	2 10 0	**Fairy Tales Told Again**	0 5 0
Purgatorio and Paradiso	2 10 0		

Cassell, Petter, Galpin & Co.: Ludgate Hill, London; Paris; and New York.

The Encyclopædic Dictionary. By ROBERT HUNTER, M.A., F.G.S., Mem. Bibl. Archæol. Soc., &c. A New and Original Work of Reference to all the Words in the English Language, with a Full Account of their Origin, Meaning, Pronunciation, and Use. Three Divisional Volumes now ready, price 10s. 6d. each. Divisions I. and II. can also be had bound in One Volume, in half-morocco, 21s.

Library of English Literature. Edited by Professor HENRY MORLEY. With Illustrations taken from Original MSS., &c. Each Vol. complete in itself.

VOL. I. SHORTER ENGLISH POEMS. 12s. 6d.
VOL. II. ILLUSTRATIONS OF ENGLISH RELIGION. 11s. 6d.
VOL. III. ENGLISH PLAYS. 11s. 6d.
VOL. IV. SHORTER WORKS IN ENGLISH PROSE. 11s. 6d.
VOL. V. LONGER WORKS IN ENGLISH VERSE AND PROSE. 11s. 6d.

Dictionary of English Literature. Being a Comprehensive Guide to English Authors and their Works. By W. DAVENPORT ADAMS. 720 pages, extra fcap. 4to, cloth, 10s. 6d.

A First Sketch of English Literature. By Professor HENRY MORLEY. Crown 8vo, 912 pages, cloth, 7s. 6d.

Dictionary of Phrase and Fable. Giving the Derivation, Source, or Origin of 20,000 Words that have a Tale to Tell. By Rev. Dr. BREWER. *Enlarged and Cheaper Edition*, cloth, 3s. 6d.; superior binding, leather back, 4s. 6d.

Popular Educator, Cassell's. *New and thoroughly Revised Edition.* Vols. I., II., and III., price 5s. each. (To be completed in Six Vols.)

The Royal Shakspere. A Handsome Fine-Art Edition of the Poet's Works. Vol. I. contains Exquisite Steel Plates and Wood Engravings. The Text is that of Prof. Delius, and the Work contains Mr. FURNIVALL's Life of Shakspere. Price 15s.

The Leopold Shakspere. The Poet's Works in Chronological Order, and an Introduction by F. J. FURNIVALL. With about 400 Illustrations. Small 4to, cloth, 6s.; cloth gilt, 7s. 6d.

Cassell's Illustrated Shakespeare. Edited by CHARLES and MARY COWDEN CLARKE. With 600 Illustrations by H. C. SELOUS. Three Vols., cloth gilt, £3 3s.

Figure Painting in Water Colours. With Sixteen Coloured Plates from Original Designs by BLANCHE MACARTHUR and JENNIE MOORE. 7s. 6d.

Flower Painting in Water Colours. With Twenty Fac-simile Coloured Plates by F. E. HULME. Crown 4to, 5s.

Sketching from Nature in Water Colours. By AARON PENLEY. With Illustrations in Chromo-Lithography, after Original Water-colour Drawings. Super-royal 4to, cloth, 15s.

Morocco: its People and Places: By EDMONDO DE AMICIS. Translated by C. ROLLIN TILTON. With nearly 200 Original Illustrations. Extra crown 4to, *Cheap Edition*, cloth, 7s. 6d.

Our Own Country. An Illustrated Geographical and Historical Description of the Chief Places of Interest in Great Britain. Vols. I., II., III., IV., and V., with upwards of 200 Illustrations in each, 7s. 6d. each.

Old and New Edinburgh, Cassell's. Vols. I. and II., with nearly 200 Original Illustrations in each, specially executed for the Work. In crown 4to, cloth, 9s. each.

The International Portrait Gallery. In Two Vols., each containing 20 Portraits in Colours, executed in the best style of Chromo-Lithography, with Memoirs. Demy 4to, cloth gilt, 12s. 6d. each; or in One Vol., 21s.

The National Portrait Gallery. Complete in Four Volumes, each containing 20 Portraits, printed in the best style of Chromo-Lithography, with Memoirs. Cloth gilt, 12s. 6d. each; or Two Double Vols., 21s. each.

Science for All. Complete in Five Vols. Edited by Dr. ROBERT BROWN, M.A., F.L.S., &c., assisted by Eminent Scientific Writers. Each containing about 350 Illustrations. Extra crown 4to, cloth, 9s. each.

Great Industries of Great Britain. With about 400 Illustrations. Extra crown 4to, 960 pages. Complete in Three Vols., cloth, 7s. 6d. each. Library binding, Three Vols. in One, 15s.

The Field Naturalist's Handbook. By the Rev. J. G. WOOD and THEODORE WOOD. Cloth, 5s.

The Races of Mankind. By ROBERT BROWN, M.A., Ph.D., F.L.S., F.R.G.S. Complete in Four Vols., containing upwards of 500 Illustrations. Extra crown 4to, cloth gilt, 6s. per Vol.

The Sea: its Stirring Story of Adventure, Peril, and Heroism. By F. WHYMPER. Complete in Four Vols., each containing 100 Original Illustrations, 4to, 7s. 6d. each. Library binding, Two Vols., 25s.

Illustrated Readings. Comprising a choice Selection from the English Literature of all Ages. With about 400 Illustrations. Two Vols., cloth, 7s. 6d.; gilt edges, 10s. 6d. each.

The Practical Dictionary of Mechanics. Containing 15,000 Drawings, with Comprehensive and TECHNICAL DESCRIPTION of each Subject. Three Vols., cloth, £3 3s.; half morocco, £3 15s.

The Countries of the World. By ROBERT BROWN, M.A., Ph.D., F.L.S., F.R.G.S. Complete in Six Vols., with about 750 Illustrations, 4to, 7s. 6d. each. Library binding, Three Vols., 37s. 6d.

Peoples of the World. Vol. I. By Dr. ROBERT BROWN. With numerous Illustrations. Price 7s. 6d.

Cities of the World. Vol. I. Illustrated throughout with fine Illustrations and Portraits. Extra crown 4to, cloth gilt, 7s. 6d.

Sports and Pastimes, Cassell's Book of. With more than 800 Illustrations, and Coloured Frontispiece. 768 pages, large crown 8vo, cloth, gilt edges, 7s. 6d.

In-door Amusements, Card Games, and Fireside Fun, Cassell's Book of. With numerous Illustrations. 224 pp., large crown 8vo, cloth, gilt edges, 3s. 6d.

The Family Physician. A Modern Manual of Domestic Medicine. By PHYSICIANS and SURGEONS of the Principal London Hospitals. Royal 8vo, cloth, 21s.

The Domestic Dictionary. An Encyclopædia for the Household. Illustrated throughout. 1,280 pages, royal 8vo, *Cheap Edition*, price 7s. 6d.

Cassell's Dictionary of Cookery. The Largest, Cheapest, and Best Book of Cookery. With 9,000 Recipes, and numerous Illustrations. *Cheap Edition*, price 7s. 6d.

Cassell's Household Guide. *New and Revised Edition.* With Illustrations on nearly every page, and Coloured Plates. Complete in Four Vols., 6s. each.

Choice Dishes at Small Cost. Containing Practical Directions to success in Cookery, and Original Recipes for Appetising and Economical Dishes. By A. G. PAYNE. 3s. 6d.

A Year's Cookery. Giving Dishes for Breakfast, Luncheon, and Dinner for Every Day in the Year, with Practical Instructions for their Preparation. By PHILLIS BROWNE. *Cheap Edition*, cloth, 3s. 6d.

What Girls Can Do. A Book for Mothers and Daughters. By PHILLIS BROWNE, Author of "A Year's Cookery," &c. Crown 8vo, cloth, *Cheap Edition*, 3s. 6d.

☛ **Cassell, Petter, Galpin & Co.'s Complete Catalogue.** *containing a List of Several Hundred Volumes, including Bibles and Religious Works, Fine-Art Volumes, Children's Books, Dictionaries, Educational Works, Handbooks and Guides, History, Natural History, Household and Domestic Treatises, Science, Serials, Travels, &c. &c., sent post free on application.*

Cassell, Petter, Galpin & Co.: Ludgate Hill, London; Paris; and New York.